BUTTERFLIES AND SECOND CHANCES

Butterflies *and*

Second Chances

A Mom's Memoir of
Love and Loss

Annette Hines

LIONCREST

PUBLISHING

BUTTERFLIES AND SECOND CHANCES

A Mom's Memoir of Love and Loss

ISBN   978-1-5445-0299-1 *Hardcover*

978-1-5445-1266-2 *Paperback*

978-1-5445-1265-5 *Ebook*

Contents

Prologue

A DAY OF RECKONING

"Why isn't she crying?"

At first, no one answered me. It didn't help that I couldn't see what was going on; they had put up a curtain for the C-section. I knew my daughter was somewhere in the other corner of the room, but I couldn't see what the doctors were doing with her. And I wasn't hearing any noises or baby sounds. But having never given birth before, I didn't know how unusual that was.

Finally, somebody told me they were putting in a breathing tube. That's why there hadn't been any crying: apparently, she couldn't breathe. I was also told her Apgar score was four. The number meant nothing to me. Four out of what? Out of four? Out of ten? A hundred? I've always liked numbers, but had no idea what this one represented in the scheme of things, what it was measuring.

Well, this is kind of absurd, I thought. But before I had a chance to ask for an explanation, there she was—my baby, being wheeled out of the delivery room. I barely saw her as she rolled by.

I didn't get to see or hold her for another eight hours.

Elizabeth was born eleven weeks early. I didn't think it was a good idea for her to be delivered so early. But the doctors said it was imperative. I had been going in every week for "stress tests," and at twenty weeks, they'd put me on bed rest because she wasn't growing. From then on, they'd monitored her closely, and when I'd come in for this most recent appointment, they'd decided they needed to deliver her right then and there. She was in distress. Something was wrong with her heart rate, and there had been very little movement in my belly over the past couple days. Things hadn't felt right, I told them. It was too quiet in there. That made them nervous.

"We always trust a mother's instincts," they reassured me. I wanted to yell at them that I wasn't a mom yet and I didn't know anything. They shouldn't trust my instincts! What did *they* want to do?

Turns out, one thing they wanted to do was have a C-section, which admittedly upset me. I asked why I couldn't be induced, and they said it would take too long and put even more stress on the baby. With induction, the contractions are stronger, and it would have been too hard on her.

"Okay, well let me call my husband," I said, "So we can talk this over with him."

They told me there was no time to wait or discuss. I could go ahead and call him and tell him to come, but this was happening *now*. I couldn't reach Wayne anyway; he was out looking at some property somewhere. I left a message on the voicemail in the family business office—this was back in 1996, before we had cell phones—telling them they needed to find Wayne and let him know that I was about to have the baby and he needed to come to the hospital.

I did manage to reach Wayne's dad, my father-in-law, who was so calming and sweet to me, always with such a soothing voice. I needed it. I was panicked, desperate for somebody to come and be with me. *I can't do this by myself*, I thought. I was so unprepared for it all. I hadn't even taken my birthing classes yet. I was actually all signed-up for them, ready to go. Geared up to excel like usual—acing my classes is *what I do*. But then, I never got the chance. The baby came early. Very early.

Wayne made it to the birth just in time, but it didn't matter because they took Elizabeth away immediately. It had all been *rush, rush, rush*—a whirlwind of signing papers, being swept down the hall, my clothes stripped off, strangers pouring into the room, and then a whole team of twenty or more attending to the baby. All the commotion made me even more panicked. Then, minutes later, they were whisking Elizabeth away. Wayne wanted to go and check on her, but they told him they were doing "procedures," and we wouldn't be able to see her for a while, so he should just stay with me.

None of my family could get there in time from Massachusetts; no one was expecting the baby to come so soon. We didn't have a crib yet. I wanted Wayne to handle things and take charge of the situation—to tell me what was going on and what I needed to do. I wanted him to calm me down and say everything was going to be okay. But he did none of that. He was just very, very quiet. He didn't step up in the way I expected him to, the way I always pictured my husband doing.

We'd only been married nine months at that point, and maybe I didn't know him very well yet. It was certainly a foreshadowing of what the next few years of parenting with him would be like; he just didn't know what to do. It had started off well. Wayne had been great in many ways. First, he was so excited when I got pregnant, just looking forward to being a dad. Then, when the doctors had put me on bed rest, and I was forced to quit my job, he worked a second job to take up the slack. He was taking care of things, and I appreciated him for that. Work was something he knew he could do, a way he could help, a language he was familiar with, his comfort zone.

But then, the day of Elizabeth's birth, I started to see this different side of him. He turned quiet. It was like he just went dark on me. It marked the beginning of my seeing how fragile my husband really was, of losing faith in him. It all started the day of her birth—but it wasn't until many hours later, in the middle of the night, that I was finally allowed to see Elizabeth. The nurses wheeled me to the NICU (Neonatal Intensive Care Unit). Until that point, I had had no idea what was going on. Nobody had given me any information. All I knew was that my daughter was on a ventilator, and she was *really* small—only two pounds.

Also, she had hair all over her—"lanugo," they called it. She looked like a little monkey. I was horrified, to be honest. I kept waiting for the motherly instinct to flood over me, but it never came. I definitely didn't look at Elizabeth and say, "Oh, my baby, I love you so much."

It wasn't like in the TV commercials—you know, the ones where the baby gets wrapped in a blanket and placed on the mom's chest and Mom just falls instantly in love with her new child. That's how I thought childbirth would be. I had all these false expectations that I would get my own beautiful Hallmark moment, like on TV.

In reality, I had none of that. All I could think to myself was, *I'm not feeling this, I'm just numb.* Elizabeth looked like a monkey, and not a cute one either. She had tubes and needles all over. When were the doctors going to remove that stuff? I had no idea. The whole situation was just like what I'd been experiencing the past few weeks coming in for stress tests: I constantly felt in the dark. Nobody had told me that my baby might be premature, that she might be born at only twenty-nine weeks, that I might have to have a C-section, that there were all these risks, that she might not be doing well. I certainly didn't expect not to be able to see her and hold her after they took her out of me. I just wasn't prepared for any of it. I didn't know the half of it.

How could this happen to me? I was twenty-eight years old. I had made all the right choices. Having grown up in poverty, I'd always had a plan in life—determined from a very early age to make myself a success and create the kind of future that I wanted. Suddenly, I was at a loss. All my intentions had gone out the window. I didn't know what to do. But I was still hopeful. I still thought I was going to get my Hallmark moment, my bonding moment with my baby. "It will be OK," I told myself. It would all pass at some point and then I would be able to take her home. Then my real life would start. Not this crazy thing that had happened to me in the hospital, but my *real life* that was promised me, the one I had always dreamed about.

These were the thoughts racing through my head as they wheeled me back up to my room. When we got there, it was right next to the bright nursery where all the healthy babies were staying. I couldn't bear to look. It was like getting hit in the face with a board. And when I think back now, twenty-two years later, to that day when Elizabeth was born, I still feel the force of that painful blow.

Little did I know how crazy things would soon become.

Five days later, I left the hospital. Without Elizabeth. Anyone who's ever had to leave the hospital without their baby will understand just how very strange it is.

She was in the NICU for the next nine weeks, and I visited every day. Wayne rarely came with me. His family didn't visit. I didn't know what I was supposed to do with this tiny baby hooked up to all these tubes. Yes, I had the nurses. They were teaching me how to take care of her, how to pump my breastmilk and prepare a bottle, how to give a bath to a two-pound baby. But the routine frustrated me in the same way I had been frustrated by my dealings with the doctors: these were things in *their* comfort zone, things *they* wanted to talk about. What about the conversations that *weren't* happening? What about knowing how to look for signs of brain injuries, blindness, missing developmental milestones?

At the time, I couldn't have known about these missing conversations. I didn't know what I didn't know. Instead, I just felt really lost. I was stuck in a kind of holding pattern or loop, waiting for all this weird stuff to finally end so that I could do what I was supposed to be doing—being a mom.

CHAPTER ONE

Here She Is

The day I took Elizabeth home from the hospital, she was only four pounds. Had she still been in the womb, it would have been thirty-eight weeks (far into the third trimester, when babies usually weigh in at around six pounds).

All I wanted was to feed her and help her grow. Those were the instructions: "She just needs to grow at this point," said the doctor nonchalantly. "Feed, grow, rest, that's it." But it wasn't so easy. Elizabeth had a weak suck; breastfeeding wasn't going well. On my part, it was hard to develop milk, given that she hadn't been with me for the first nine weeks. I wasn't producing enough, and she wasn't latching on right.

I had visited Elizabeth every day, all day, at the NICU. I would try to nurse her when she was able, and also pump. The nurses had been very helpful and assured me everything would be easier once Elizabeth got bigger—and especially once she was out of the hospital and home with me. I would be more relaxed there, they said. For now, I just needed to concentrate on drinking lots of water, eating right, and getting good sleep.

They really believed that was all we were going to need. Or maybe they didn't—I guess I'll never know for sure. But when I think back to that time, I always remember them as kind and supportive. I appreciated that they had given me specific things to do. It had made me start to feel like I had a plan again. Or at least I had *strived* to feel that way. I had possessed a new sense of purpose, had been reading all the baby books, making sure everything was ready for when I finally got to bring Elizabeth home.

But now here we were, finally out of the hospital, and the breastfeeding stuff was still driving me crazy. *Why wasn't this working?* As if leaving my baby in the NICU for two months hadn't been stressful enough, now I had to worry about something as seemingly simple as breastfeeding. I felt guilty, like I was doing it wrong.

Argh, the truth was that nothing was going according to plan. Not according to all the books I had been reading, that's for sure. What was I going to do? Failure was not an option. This wasn't some small thing I was struggling with: I was trying to *feed my baby*. What could be more elemental than that? I *had* to figure it out. I was driven to action. But also so frustrated. *What is your problem, Annie? You can't even get THIS right?* How did this happen? I was good at, literally, everything else. Why wasn't I good at this? I felt stupid. Mad at myself. Demoralized.

And yet...I loved being a mom. I loved her beautiful blue eyes. Her bald head. She smelled so good. I wanted to sniff her up all day long. And I was just so happy now to have her home. My favorite thing was taking her out for walks in the stroller. After nine weeks of visiting her every day in the hospital, it just felt so good to be out in the sunshine together, with the warm rays on my face. I also loved sitting in my rocking chair and rocking her back and forth. I was just happy to be home, like a normal family. I could finally relax and take a breath.

Yes, she was fussy. She spat up a lot. But mostly she slept, as babies do. I'd watch her dozing peacefully and feel such joy to be her mom and finally have her close to me. I couldn't put her down. I held her so much all day that no laundry or other chores got done. Not that I wanted to do that stuff anyway. Housekeeping was the last thing on my mind.

Because she was still so small, she slept in a little basket that Wayne's cousin Pauline had let us borrow. It was adorable—lined with pretty fabric, like something out of an Ann Geddes photograph. Wayne and I had also bought a crib, but it was way too early for that. She was tiny. She didn't fit into any clothes, even the preemie outfits. We struggled to find diapers small enough. Someone even suggested that we try doll clothes—which we considered but never followed through with.

I knew from the doctors and all the books I had been reading that she was going to be behind. As a preemie, it was going to take a while for her to catch up. But she would get there; we just needed to give her time. We were one of the lucky ones. In the NICU, we had been in a pod of six babies, two had died while we were there. One of the moms had lost two of her three triplets. More days than not, there had been a crisis in the ward with one of the babies or another. You learned not to ask when a baby was no longer in their bed. Had they been moved? Sent home? Or the worst? Better not to ask.

We had gotten one of those terrible calls from the doctors, too. It was back when Elizabeth was still only ten days old. I was at home, getting ready to come in to the hospital for my visit. I couldn't wait to see her. That day, they would bring her out of her *isolette* (incubator) and let me hold her skin-to-skin on my chest. They called this Koala Care, just like those adorable little animals from the other side of the world: good for the baby and good for mommy, too. So I had been at home feeling excited when the doctors called and told me to rush over. Elizabeth was in trouble.

We found out later that she had crashed, stopped breathing. They had to restart her heart. She had already been on a ventilator. But they had saved her. I got the priest from our church to come in and baptize her right there in the hospital. I wanted her to be safe no matter what happened. It felt good to make some choices. I felt in control for that moment.

Eventually, they would send us home with her and tell us everything would be fine. She was very strong, they told me. She just needed to sleep and eat and grow, they would say. She would catch up in time. We believed it all. We thought the worst had passed and we were done— now Elizabeth was going to be fine. Knowledge is power, I told myself, and as long as I could understand what was going on, things would be okay. So I devoured all the baby books: I wanted to know week-by-week what to look for with Elizabeth's development.

I'm the person who needs to understand everything. I had learned early on that anything could be studied and mastered, with enough preparation. Growing up on welfare in a single-parent household does that to you. You do what it takes to make sure you'll always be in control of your destiny. It was no different now. I told myself that things were going to work out. And, for a while, they did.

Thinking back to Elizabeth's baptism, four weeks after I brought her home from the hospital, it's almost possible for me to imagine an alternate reality where everything was hunky-dory and life as a mom was what I had always envisioned.

The baptism was a beautiful event. Although Elizabeth had already been baptized by our priest in the hospital, this was our opportunity to have the entire ceremony of baptism. Ceremonies are so important as a rite of passage in life. They mark those special moments—and Elizabeth's baptism was exactly that for me. We had it at our church, which had been very supportive of us. My mom and my sister and Wayne's family were all there. It had been hard to find a baptismal dress that would fit Elizabeth. The one we put on her was very big, but it worked out fine. My sister and her husband were the godparents. I remember there were a lot of babies at the church being baptized that day. A big year for new babies, apparently, which made it feel like even more of a big festive moment for me. Here, Elizabeth looked like all the other babies except a little smaller.

After the ceremony, we threw a little party at our apartment. Everybody was there, including my mom and

Wayne's family. It felt good. Celebratory. Like everybody just took a breath and agreed it would all be fine.

Within a few months, life would look very different.

A HOUSE IS NOT A HOME

Not long after the baptism, Wayne and I sold our one-room condo and bought a house so that we could have a little more room. I had hoped that life with Elizabeth would be easier in the bigger space. I painted her room yellow because it was sunny and bright, and put up curtains. I decorated it with Winnie the Pooh. What can I say? I set to nesting: learned how to plant a garden, how to make cheesecake (harder than it looks, it takes twelve hours in the fridge to set). I made friends with neighbors across the way. Had dinner parties. Went for walks by the river.

Nesting felt good. But it didn't last long. When Elizabeth was five or six months old, she started to cry. A lot. I couldn't get her to eat solid food. She threw up all the time. It was weird: something about her just seemed uncomfortable and not right. Then I noticed she wasn't sitting up or lifting her head. I knew from my baby books what I should be looking for in terms of development. And I knew things weren't going according to plan.

As readers may have picked up by now, I'm someone who

craves knowledge, who needs to understand it *all*. Give me a problem, I've always said, and I will solve it. With enough preparation, I can learn and master anything.

Or so I thought.

I could tell there was more going on with Elizabeth than just the typical preemie issues. It wasn't just that she was acting like a three-month old at five months. She literally couldn't hold her head up. And there was something wrong with her sight. She wasn't really *looking* at things. It was hard for her to focus on me, and one of her eyes seemed to be turned inward.

Then there was the crying. I knew babies could be colicky, but this? She would wail for literally hours on end. I did my best to stay calm and collected, but honestly there were days when I thought I'd lose my mind from all the screaming. One time, I ran out of diapers and had to take her to the local Walmart, where we ended up waiting in line forever because something was wrong at the register. Of course, Elizabeth was screaming the whole time. She had been screaming so long that I had just gone numb. Then, a woman in line started yelling at me to do something about my crying baby: "Hold her, pick her up, do *something*!"

In hindsight I get why it must have looked weird, with

Elizabeth sill in the carriage crying her head off. But what this judgmental lady didn't realize was that there was nothing more I *could* do. I had tried everything: picked her up, soothed her, fed her, gave her a blanket. I was out of ideas. I knew I needed to bring Elizabeth back to the doctor to reconvene and figure out what to do next. But at that moment, I was just out of ideas. My baby wouldn't stop crying no matter what. I felt so helpless and useless. I just grabbed my diapers and got out of there. It was all I could do.

This can't be normal, I thought to myself. *There MUST be something wrong.* Or was it just me? I had no one else to give me an objective second opinion. I was just so alone and isolated at this time that it was hard to think clearly.

It wasn't until my mom came down to visit and see the new house that someone else finally voiced concerns. I remember Elizabeth was sitting in the baby swing (which was the only thing that calmed her down), screaming her head off as usual. She wouldn't eat. She threw up her bottle. It was the typical craziness. But this time, my mom was there. She was looking intently at Elizabeth, but not saying anything.

My mom had been helpful, putting up curtains and cleaning things, but also there was a lot going on under the surface with her. All things being equal, I was grateful that she had come and taken care of things, made me food, mom stuff. But she had also been observing the household, observing Elizabeth.

Finally, we talked, and she said out loud all the things I had been thinking: "Elizabeth can't sit up yet," "she's not grabbing things," "there's something going on," "she's missing all of the milestones." I don't know if those were her exact words, but the gist of it was she was concerned. On the one hand, it was a relief to hear. I wasn't crazy. My suspicions about Elizabeth were valid and appropriate. On the other hand, deep down I still didn't want to believe anything was wrong. I wanted to explain it all away: "No, it's just reflux, a lot of preemies get it." That's what the doctors had said, after all, and they had put Elizabeth on reflux medicine. It was probably just the medicine that was making her so irritable. Right? That must be it.

Oh, how I wanted to believe that. But if I'm being totally honest, even back then I knew it wasn't true. Maybe if it had just been the crying, the theory would have held up. But it didn't explain all the rest. Why wasn't she looking at me? Why wasn't she sitting up? Why wasn't she grabbing for things? I suppose there was still a small measure of plausible deniability at that point. I could still hem and haw and rationalize. I could trust in the professionals and their expertise over my own parental instincts; it was easier that way—and it was good while it lasted.

But then, at about six or seven months, the seizures started.

A TERRIFYING NEW STAGE

At first, I didn't know what they were. These weren't the obvious seizures where somebody flops to the ground and shakes all over. It was more like a strange bowing or praying motion. Elizabeth's legs and arms would come in toward one another, then a few seconds later, the same. The duration of the episodes varied, but generally, they lasted about twenty to thirty seconds.

When I tried to describe the strange movements to Elizabeth's doctor, he said it was probably nothing and sent me home. So I made an appointment with a developmental pediatrician whom we had seen before, but he also waved it away: he still blamed it on reflux and said the spasm was just her tensing up and feeling pain from the acid.

Over the next few days, the seizures got more severe. And more frequent. Worst of all, I could tell Elizabeth was aware of what was going on while she was having them. She would scream and look terrified. It was devastating to see her like that. All I could do was put her down and make sure she wasn't vomiting. I was freaking out, and Wayne thought I had lost my mind!

Finally, we took her to the emergency room, and Elizabeth seized in front of the doctors, over and over again. The look on their faces was not good. They ordered both an MRI and CAT scan, which showed that Elizabeth had injuries to two different parts of her brain. The doctors said they were preemie birth injuries, otherwise known as CP hypoxia. CP stands for cerebral palsy, which means damage was done to the developing brain before the child was born, or sometimes during the birth itself.

After studying the MRI, one neurologist told me that Elizabeth's brain looked like Swiss cheese, with holes everywhere. To this day, I shudder when I recall those words. How could he have said something so awful and insensitive? I guess he thought he was trying to be helpful by giving me a visual. No thanks.

Ultimately, the doctors diagnosed Elizabeth with something called "infantile spasms," which sounds rather benign but is actually a lot more serious than your average seizure disorder.

After getting the diagnosis, we had to stay in the hospital for a few days while the doctors tried to control the seizures, which were coming more frequently now. Every time Elizabeth would have one, we'd ring the bell for the nurse. But because it was a "teaching hospital," we'd get not just the doctor but a whole group of people, sometimes a dozen of them, coming in to look and learn. I guess Elizabeth was an "interesting" case, not something they saw every day. Good for them. But to me, it felt rude. Like we were on display. At the time, I didn't know I could refuse the peanut gallery. I wish someone had *told* me I had the option to say no. How are patients supposed to know these things?

No one ever told me what the plan was or what we were going to do to try to "fix" Elizabeth. There had to be something we could do, I kept telling them. And that's how I thought about it at the time: as *fixing* not *managing*. "There must be some medication," I would say to them, "some kind of surgery. How are you going to stop the seizures from happening?" It was just like when Elizabeth was born and nobody seemed to be able to tell me what was going on, why she wasn't crying. Here I was in the same situation, and again, I felt in the dark. I wasn't asking for much. I just wanted some information—someone to *talk* to me and explain what was happening, what it all meant.

But they couldn't. I didn't understand it then, but I do now. The reason the doctors couldn't tell me what to expect—what this meant for Elizabeth in the long run— is that, frankly, there *are* no predictions. With CP and seizure disorders, and other neurological and developmental conditions, it's different for everyone. A lot of kids go on to build skills and achieve. A lot don't. Time to throw out the *What to Expect* books (yes, I had bought them all!): they no longer applied to us.

Was Elizabeth going to walk someday? Was she going to talk? They didn't know.

One thing they *were* able to tell me, for better or worse, was that she was partially blind. They called it cortical visual impairment, which is common in kids with brain injuries. It meant that her blindness, or "low vision," was not due to an injury to her visual system but rather her brain: she couldn't see properly because her brain wasn't able to read the signals. Her sight—what little she had— fluctuated greatly, which is common with this kind of condition. Sometimes, the child is able to see a lot. But then, the next day, their vision may completely shut down, and they can't see anything. This is especially true when a child is sick and their brain and body are busy responding to it.

I couldn't believe no one had identified Elizabeth's blindness earlier on, when she was at the NICU. Now that I've learned more about retinopathy of prematurity—and how common it is in babies like her—I'm baffled that nobody at the hospital would have thought to test her vision. I just don't get it.

Would that same mistake happen today? I hope not. It

was a long time ago. And, in many ways, those experiences I had when Elizabeth was a baby feel like ancient history, water under the bridge. That's how it feels *now*. Back *then*, all I could think was, *what the *&^% is wrong with these people?* It was starting to make me mad.

MY ANGER GROWS

Every step of the way, it seemed the doctors had been getting it wrong. Worse, they had been doing it in a manner that dismissed me and my (apparently justified!) concerns. First, there was the pediatrician, who thought it was all nothing. Then, the developmental pediatrician, who thought it was just reflex. And then, the neurologist—at least he had finally given me a diagnosis, but he couldn't help adding in that terrible Swiss cheese comment.

Wasn't there anyone who could just provide an actual *plan*? Sure, every situation is different, and the odds may be tough—but at least if there's a strategy, there's a possibility of a solution. That's what bothered me the most. I felt so powerless in the face of the great unknown. I am a process-oriented person. If there's a problem, I like to know what the options are and what steps are being taken to address it. But without any semblance of a plan, I grew increasingly frustrated.

It didn't help that we had to share a hospital room with

an older teenager with disabilities. She was in a wheel-chair, no speech, wearing diapers, constantly drooling. *This is what Elizabeth is going to look like*, I thought. *This is our future.*

Then, there was the girl's mom, who looked old and haggard. In reality, she was probably only ten years older than me, maybe fifteen. But she looked ancient. All frazzled and gray, her hair unkempt, her face wrinkled. She looked like life had beaten her down. She didn't smile and was not friendly to me and Elizabeth.

The whole scene was a foreshadowing, and it horrified me. I felt like throwing up. Did the hospital really have to do that? Put a baby and a teenager in the same room? It doesn't make any sense. Would a doctor have a newly diagnosed child with autism go out and meet an autistic twenty-five-year old? It made me angry. The writing was on the wall with Elizabeth, but nobody seemed to want to tell me the truth. Here I was, surrounded by doctors, dozens of them, all these accomplished medical professionals who found my daughter and her condition so fascinating in their clinical way—but where was the support?

It was a turning point. What was I going to do? The doctors didn't have a plan. Wayne certainly didn't have a plan. He had gone to most of the doctor's appointments but hadn't seemed to absorb any of the information. He had also become very frustrated with Elizabeth's crying. It was like he lacked all natural instincts. He just never knew what the right thing to do was.

It's not like anybody was telling *me* what to do. But some things just come instinctively. I don't buy that only moms have parental instincts. Dads have it in them, too—this capacity to be with kids and bond and just do what's needed. But Wayne didn't have that gene. It worried me a lot. It wasn't that he was cold or callous; he just *couldn't* do it. Then again, I didn't grow up with a dad. I had no experience as to what that looked like. Perhaps I was being too hard on him. But my emotions were whirling around like a tornado. and that was truly how I felt at the time: alone.

It was going to be all up to me. Time to take matters into my own hands. Everything I had mapped out for my life had changed. What was my new plan? How was I going to save Elizabeth? I had to do whatever it took for my daughter. It wasn't about me anymore. Elizabeth was my everything; I was deeply in love with her. I know it sounds weird to put it in those terms, in the language of romance, but it's the closest I can come to describing the intensity of my emotions. It was a physical thing, like the passionate rush, the flood of feelings and hormones, that happens when you first fall in love with someone.

And I felt it stronger than ever then, especially after those first few months—which, in retrospect, had been a period of happiness and joy, even though she had cried a lot. Before the seizures started, I had still been able to see Elizabeth as my perfect baby. But now, my love toward her was combined with an equally fierce streak of resentment—at the doctors, Wayne, God—for taking that "perfect baby" feeling away and not helping to replace it with something, some sort of *plan* for this new reality, new world, that had suddenly, violently come into being.

I was overcome by a parental instinct to protect her. She didn't ask or deserve to be wrenched into this chaotic unknown. It all just felt so cruel. Wasn't there some medicine she could take, or some treatment, or some surgery? If the so-called experts didn't know how to fix the problem, or even try to fix it, then why was I trusting or listening to them? Did I really have to hand over my kid's future to these people who never seemed to have any solutions?

It was time for me to start searching for my own answers.

TAKING MATTERS INTO MY OWN HANDS

There was fervor in my newfound anger. I was ready to make changes. But the more I learned about infantile spasms, the more I realized how much of an uphill battle we were up against. We had a clear diagnosis now. But what we were seeing with Elizabeth's seizures was not promising.

We had tried medicine after medicine to get the seizures under control. First, there was something called ACTH, a hormone which required us to inject her every day for three to four weeks. Brutal. Imagine having to stick a needle into your own kid. Initially, the insurance company wouldn't pay for a nurse to come out and do it. But I flat-out refused to do it myself, and for some reason, nobody expected Wayne to do it—not the doctor, not the insurance company.

I don't like needles, and I just couldn't do it. Couldn't stick her. So eventually the insurance company gave in. They sent nurses to come give the shots. The nurses were very sweet and pretty much my only company for those weeks that Elizabeth was on ACTH.

I think of that story often because it was my very first experiment with medical advocacy, the first example of me saying, "No, I'm *not* doing that, this is *not* how it's going to be"—and then having a successful resolution.

But in terms of Elizabeth and her health, there was no success. No improvement by the end of the treatment period. So we moved on to another medication. And then another. All the medications have serious side effects, from sleepiness to permanent impact on intelligence and everything in between. She hated the medicine and spat most of it up. I'm sure it tasted awful. It was hard to figure out whether she was getting the right dose of anything. So much of it felt like guessing.

It was such a scary time, and within a few months, her seizures had evolved from the kind of spasms I described earlier to the more generalized, tonic-clonic, or what they call grand mal, seizures. This was a bad sign. Among kids who are diagnosed with infantile spasms, generally the earlier they start having seizures, and the earlier those seizures evolve into bigger ones, the worse the forecast.

It was a lot of scary information. But there was one bright spot during this time. The only person in the hospital who had actually given me some helpful, concrete advice had been the social worker on staff who had directed me to various therapeutic resources. At her recommendation, we were able to procure, through our insurance company, early intervention (EI) services. (Back then, the state of Virginia wouldn't pay for EI—but if your insurance provider offered this benefit, you were in luck.)

So we went, me and Elizabeth, two mornings a week. It wasn't perfect: they didn't come to our house like they do in other parts of the country. But it was something. I took

Elizabeth to the early intervention center for occupational therapy (OT) and physical therapy (PT), and they also had a playgroup there. She seemed to really like going. She would smile and engage more than I had ever seen her do before. She loved Circle Time, where the group would sing songs like "The Wheels on the Bus"—and I loved singing to her. My voice could crash a train, but Elizabeth seemed to like listening to Mommy, so I sang to her all the time back then. I loved being able to make her smile!

Then there was the physical therapist, who was just wonderful with her, working with her on standing, rolling, and moving. Of course, Elizabeth was not able to do any of these things on her own. But the PT was helping her build up her muscles. And Elizabeth loved to move. It was so clear to me that she was a fighter and she wanted to learn. She did everything that was asked of her with a huge smile on her face, and she knew when she was accomplishing her goals.

It was all so great for her—and for mommy.

SEEING BUTTERFLIES

I remember one day, as Elizabeth and I were heading across the parking lot and into the EI building, a beautiful butterfly kept fluttering around her. As far as I can remember, this was the first time the butterfly thing had happened. But it would become a real theme with her.

I don't know what it was about Elizabeth and butterflies, but I wasn't the only one who noticed it. She had a connection with them; they were drawn to her like they are to light. She just adored everything about butterflies: butterfly pictures, stories, songs, and more. When she got a little older, the butterflies would land on her arm and stay there—she loved the sensation on her skin and would giggle every time.

I guess it's appropriate that the first butterfly moment happened at the EI center. It was a magical place for her, and it marked the beginning of a hopeful new stage. Elizabeth also had a separate private PT appointment every week, and I remember that therapist was wonderful, too.

As for me, I was able—through the EI center and the various personnel—to finally start meeting people, special needs professionals, who were actually thoughtful and comforting. They weren't freaked out by Elizabeth, and unlike the doctors, they weren't only interested in her as a medical case study.

I took great comfort in these individuals. They kept me sane and gave me something to do. It was helping. But I still didn't really have any parents or peers in the special needs community who I could talk to. I still felt alone. I had almost no social interactions other than occasionally hanging out with Wayne's cousin, Pauline, who also had an infant around the same age. We got along great and would get together for lunch and shopping. Our babies were very different, but that never mattered. The EI center and those outings with Pauline were my life-lines—and so was church. I went to mass every week and everybody there was so nice. That certainly helped too.

Wayne himself was nowhere to be found; he was always working. He was the only one of us employed at this time, so I'm not knocking him for it, per se. But he certainly didn't help with anything related to Elizabeth. Her health issues were just too much for him to handle. He didn't know what to do with her. It all seemed to make him very nervous, so he stayed away.

All in all, when I think back to this period of my life, when Elizabeth was still an infant, I have mixed memories. Having to figure everything out on my own was tough, no doubt. But through it all, I learned a lot. It set in motion an important personal journey that continues to this day, not just as a mother but as someone who went on to help other parents and families struggling in similar situations.

For that I am grateful.

ASK QUESTIONS

If I knew what I know now back when we were still in

Virginia, I would have probably been more persistent with the doctors who kept shrugging off my concerns. Granted, there wasn't a lot of choice in the area where I lived, in terms of trying to find a second opinion. And that's a major problem in certain parts of the country. But I could have been more vocal in questioning the developmental pediatrician and others, and perhaps even asking for a second look from a different specialist.

I'm not saying I would, or should have, gone ballistic on them. Quite the opposite. It doesn't do anyone any good to raise a ruckus. You'll just get to be known as the crazy mom who shouldn't be listened to. The doctors will discount what you're saying. In my case, I probably came across as too emotional—which is understandable, but makes it all that much easier to be dismissed as a kook.

What I have learned since then is that there's a way to advocate for your child from a place of strength while still being respectful and having a productive dialogue. Of course, this is easier said than done, especially when you're in a traumatic moment and an emotionally charged state of mind. And as a special needs parent, sometimes it seems like those traumatic moments string together into a continuous emotional spinout!

I often recommend that a parent bring someone else, a trusted friend or family member, along with them to hospital visits, doctor appointments, etc. Occasionally, it can be a spouse or co-parent, as long as they are calm and collected—but usually the better choice is someone who's a bit removed from the situation.

A friend or neighbor can also help by taking notes. We all know how hard it is to remember what someone is telling us when we're upset. And no matter how hard we try to keep it together, it's natural in some of these situations— when we're in the hospital, talking to doctors, etc.—to feel raw and emotionally fragile.

I also encourage readers to make use of the hospital "resource person." Generally, there's one of these at every hospital and medical center. I can't stress this enough: they are your friend, especially in crisis situations. They are founts of knowledge and information: they know where everything is located, what's available, what insurance will and won't pay for, and much, much more.

Same with visiting nurse associations and other home-care agencies. There are all sorts of valuable resources out there. The problem, of course, is that you have to know where to find them, and have to self-identify what you need. When I was trying to navigate the system in the early years of parenting Elizabeth, I had no idea. But these tools are out there, and they can help.

For me, getting Elizabeth into EI was the first important step in my journey to educating and empowering myself as a special needs parent. EI is different from state to state, both in terms of what it consists of and who's paying. You have to do your research and find out which agency handles EI in your state. See what's offered, what the rules are, and be prepared to make a plan. The earlier you get services for your child, the better, and EI can be a good practice run for what lies ahead once your child enters the school system.

Getting Elizabeth into EI was the first time I felt like I had actually made some progress, some traction. Especially after the many months of struggling to navigate the *medical* system, being in and out of hospitals and feeling so powerless around the doctors who wouldn't give me any answers, there was a sense of relief—maybe only a small one, but it was something—when I started taking Elizabeth to the EI center and to her therapy appointments.

But I still didn't have a plan.

And, as I was starting to realize, there was only so much I could do for my daughter in the environment I was living in at that time. In the area of southern Virginia where we were, there was the EI center but not much else.

It was during this period that I started to dream of a different, better environment for Elizabeth—and for me.

CHAPTER TWO

The Big Move

"I'm moving to Boston with Elizabeth," I said to Wayne firmly.

His eyes cautiously avoided mine.

"I hope you decide to join us."

And that was that. With those words, I made it official: Elizabeth and I were leaving Virginia, with or without him. It wasn't the first time I had broached the subject with my husband. I had talked to him before and asked him what he thought about moving to Boston, but his answer was no. He definitely didn't want to leave his family—or the family business. It was the life he knew.

He had always said no. I don't think he took me very seriously the times before when I had asked about moving.

But this time, he knew something was different. I had a new conviction in my voice. He could tell I was serious.

I had always been someone who acted on instinct, and now was no different. I just knew it was the right choice. The services for Elizabeth would be better in Boston. There would be more specialists. I'd have more access to the information I needed. Most important, I'd be around people who cared about me and who would love Elizabeth. My mom was there, my sister and brother-in-law, their kids, my brother, all of my friends from high school. Even some friends from college. Not to mention the people I had worked with before I went off to law school.

When I thought about it in those terms, there really was no contest. In Boston, I'd have a community of folks I could count on. There was my friend, Beth, who was a doctor there. She and another friend, Andrea, had come down to see me after Elizabeth was born. Beth and Andrea were great—I had known them since high school, and they had even been my bridesmaids in my wedding—but they were both in Boston.

In Virginia, I didn't have any friends. There was no community, nothing. I hadn't worked long enough to *make* friends in the area. A few people from my brief work experience stayed in touch, but not for very long. We knew some people at church, which was nice. But there just wasn't anything to hold onto there. I had been so lonely the past few months. I knew I needed to get out. Husband or no husband.

Wayne *was* trying to be strong. Holding down two jobs, working nights selling windows, hustling to make money, which we definitely needed to pay our mortgage on our new house. We had bought the house before the seizures started, before we knew there was something really wrong. Now, three or four months later, it was like everything had been put on hold. The place was still barely furnished. But what I needed most was a real partner, not a sofa set.

Again, Wayne was trying to be a good provider and help in the way he knew how. But there was just no emotional support from his side. We weren't connected on that level. And it was the same with his family. They never bonded with me, or even with the baby. Maybe part of the issue was that I never really got a chance to know his family, or for them to get to know me, before Elizabeth. It was all pretty sudden: Wayne and I had met in school, but I didn't meet his family until after we got engaged. And then we had only just gotten married when the baby came so early. All of which is to say, we didn't really know each other, Wayne's family and I. Sometimes it was like being with a room full of strangers. Sounds awful, but that's how it felt.

After Elizabeth started having seizures, we invited a

group of them to our house for a big family meeting. It was Wayne's brothers, their wives, his parents, and his cousin. We wanted to let them know what was going on, to bring them into our world and all that we'd been going through. We were hoping to rally the troops, as they say.

It was also, I suppose, a cry for help. But they just didn't get it. Their reaction was strikingly cold and flat. Not mean, exactly. Just blank. There wasn't anything *there*. They simply didn't know what to say or do.

None of this is to suggest that my own family is perfect. My mom had come down to Virginia for a while and had tried to help in *her* own way, putting up curtains and things like that. She didn't always know what to say or do either. But at least she was there. And she would be there in Boston, where I'd have other family and friends I could count on.

For my own sake and for Elizabeth's, the decision to move was a no-brainer—especially with the kind of medical support Elizabeth was clearly going to need moving forward.

Over the past months, we had tried several different seizure medications before finally landing on one that seemed to have an effect. In the part of the state where we lived, there were only one or two pediatric neurology groups within 150 miles. We'd have to go to Richmond, two and a half hours away, or to Duke, in North Carolina, which was even farther.

There was nothing nearby—and at this point, I just knew that, if we stayed, the healthcare landscape wasn't going to be good enough. Not for what we were dealing with. We needed serious help. Boston had all of the specialty pediatricians. The famous Children's Hospital was there. I needed to be close to those kinds of institutions and resources. I didn't know exactly what the future would look like, but I knew I'd be able to get some direction in Boston, some help with what to do next.

God knows, I needed it. I had never been so scared.

A NEW LIFE

For better or worse, Wayne came to join us in Boston pretty much right away. It couldn't have been more than a couple weeks. He just said, "Okay, I guess I'll come." No emotion. That's Wayne.

But then we had to deal with selling the house in Virginia, which of course we had only just bought. So for a little while, Wayne was occupied with that and had to travel back and forth. But it was actually for the best that he was away so often: we were living, at the time, in my mom's small apartment in Boston, all three of us in one little room.

We were in that cramped apartment for about ten months total, during which time we sold the place in Virginia. Although we took a small loss on the house, we were still doing okay, all things considered. It didn't take long for Wayne to find new work in Boston. He had some friends he knew from Wharton, and they had a business there— so he was able to get a job with them doing some real estate work. Then, as soon as we were able, we got our own apartment in Natick, Massachusetts, just west of the city.

Things were coming together, and for the most part, it was a happy, hopeful time, even back when we were still in my mom's place. In fact, one of my favorite memories of those early days, after the move from Virginia, was celebrating Elizabeth's first birthday party in my sister's backyard. My family was there, some friends came, and all of a sudden, I realized, *wow I have a community.*

It was exactly what I had been searching for, why I had come to Boston in the first place. Looking around at my family and friends that day, I found myself beaming with happiness at the sight of all these people hugging Elizabeth, kissing her, walking her around, loving her. I remember a huge pile of presents just for her. Everybody seemed so happy to be there with her. It all just felt so nice and normal in the middle of all the craziness.

And I really got to see Elizabeth in action. She was magnetic, just drew people in. She had a way of connecting that I would soon realize was her greatest gift. People wanted to hold her and help her with anything she needed. It would serve her well through the years.

As for me, it just felt amazing to finally have some backup: I could take a break for a second if I needed to. Unlike in Virginia, I had people here who could take the baby off my hands for an hour and let me grab a nap or go for a walk. Best of all, they were family. I was around my loved ones. It was home.

I don't mean to paint an overly rosy picture. Elizabeth still screamed all the time. She was still very difficult—and of course, she still had the same medical and neurological issues.

But, and especially once we moved to Natick, there were all these great resources nearby: a neighborhood health clinic with a holistic medical program and specialized developmental pediatricians. It didn't take me long to get connected with the great people at Children's Hospital, and soon after that, the Perkins School for the Blind, which had its own early intervention program and parents' group. Even my new church, St. Patrick's in Natick, where I was now a parishioner, had a nursing program.

Within about two months, my network was in place: EI services, nurse practitioner, developmental pediatrician. I was meeting other parents; we were doing playgroup. It was everything I wanted in Virginia but couldn't find. I had found my safe space. I started to breathe again.

LETTING GO OF MY ANGER

I was happier than I'd felt in a long time, but not everyone around me had that same perception of my improved mood. Elizabeth's pediatrician, a great guy named Tom Silva, could tell I was still a bit of a neurotic mess. In particular, he noticed I had a chip on my shoulder about doctors. He was right: there *was* still an edge to me—especially when I had to take Elizabeth to the hospital.

I had good reason to be on edge. Elizabeth was still having a lot of problems during this time, throwing up a lot. In fact, pretty early on after moving to Boston, she had suffered a massive seizure that sent her to the ICU at Mass General. It was a seizure that went on for hours and hours. We only went to Mass General because it was the closest hospital. But we followed up at Children's once we moved to Natick.

The Children's Hospital in Boston turned out to play a very important role for me and my family, and in more ways than one. Tom Silva suggested (well, he kind of insisted) that I join a volunteer project that the hospital was doing. Thank God he did: it was such a good thing for me. It gave me something to do, meetings to go to, parents to organize.

From that point on, I was quickly introduced to a number of influential parents in the special needs community. One of them was a mom named Susan Nadworny, who ran something called Massachusetts Families Organizing for Change. I had heard that they did parent leadership training, and Susan invited me, so I went. Wow. That one connection led to all kinds of amazing benefits for me and Elizabeth: I learned about specialized Medicaid programs in our state, funds for critically ill children, and most importantly, advocacy as an effective tool for change.

MFOFC was a godsend for me—and all because I connected with Susan. I still remember one great conversation I had with her when I was studying for the bar exam and feeling so overwhelmed. I had been in desperate need of advice. She talked to me on the phone about my wanting to go back to work, to be a lawyer. I just found it so nice of her to give me her time. She talked to me a long while and passed along the names of two attorneys—two women who later became great mentors of mine. She also told me about her own son, James, who was ten years older than Elizabeth. Susan had definitely been at this a good deal longer than I had.

I remember she opened up to me about how difficult it was to brush James's teeth, and how her husband never seemed to get that *this*—the tooth-brushing—was the thing that made her crazy every day. No matter how long they had been married and what a great husband he was, he still drove her bonkers sometimes—and they still had an occasional disconnect around parenting issues.

Finally, here was somebody—Susan—who *got* it. That's what I thought. Someone who was honest with me about how life is just really hard sometimes, and how these little things, like tooth-brushing, can make us completely lose it. I appreciated Susan being so real with me. It made me feel so much better that I wasn't alone. Even though she was ten years ahead of me on this journey, she was still going through it. It made me realize there would always be frustrations, it was part of life, and it was okay.

Of course, she also was hugely helpful in getting me out there and facilitating my meeting other attorneys who were also special needs moms. Through Susan, I also got to know a number of other parents who were doing cool things, similar initiatives involving special needs advocacy and support. Nowadays, these programs are much more common. But, back then, they were truly groundbreaking. All in all, it was an exciting time—and, on a personal level, it gave me the opportunity, at just the right moment, to shed some of the heaviness that had been weighing me down for so long. I stopped being pissed off.

There would be more anger to come, a lot of it, in the following years—but for then, I had found my safe space, my people, my community.

PEOPLE WHO "GET IT"

One of the biggest reliefs for me was to finally be around other people, specifically in my parents' group, who just "got it." They understood my anger; I didn't have to bite my tongue around them. I often say that before I found my community, I had a bloody tongue from biting it so much.

Special needs parents always have to bend and put on a happy face so as to not make others uncomfortable. Meanwhile, *we*'re the ones going through hell. Isn't that something? I hear it time and again from the families I talk to and work with. They feel pressure to be cheery. They think nobody wants to hear their negativity. They're right.

I felt the same way: our society may pay lip service to the value of "speaking your truth," but in practice, people don't want to hear it. They're sympathetic to a degree. But certain thoughts and feelings are just a step too far; it's not socially acceptable to voice them out loud.

Thankfully, there are these safe spaces, communities, both virtual and "real," where's it okay to be ourselves, to show our pain and anger. I've never been an over-sharer or someone who wears my heart on my sleeve. But even for me, being able to talk freely and connect with other parents in these venues was incredibly liberating. It was the beginning of my processing my anger—and, ultimately, putting it aside and moving toward healing.

CHAPTER THREE

The Diagnosis

It felt like a cruel twist of fate that just as things were getting better for Elizabeth and me from a community perspective, her health was going down, down, down. We couldn't figure out what was wrong with her. By this point, thankfully, we had her seizures under control, but we couldn't get her to eat. So we had what's called a G-tube put in. It was a way to make sure we got food into her, as well as medications. The G-tube, or gastrostomy tube, goes through the abdomen and directly into the stomach.

It did help somewhat, but not long after that, she needed stomach surgery so that she would stop throwing up all the time. The procedure was called fundoplication. The operation itself was successful—she stopped throwing up and was more comfortable—but then she couldn't tolerate any food in her stomach. She was in distress.

Finally, when Elizabeth was about two and a half, we had to have a central line placed, which is an intravenous line that goes into the heart. Parenteral nutrition (TPN) was the only way to feed her. But it meant the risk of infections on the line, which could kill her. It was the right decision to do the central line—but the stakes were high.

It also required something called "sterile technique" at home, which meant that we were basically turning our home into "hospital sterile." To do medical care, you have to have a sterile environment and be trained in sterile technique. Only a few years earlier, parents would never have been allowed to do that at home. But due to pressure from the insurance companies, families now had to do more and more themselves.

The nurses at Children's had done a good job of training me, so it wasn't like I was totally unprepared. They taught me how to sterilize, and then they also watched me do it. You had to pass a kind of test before you were allowed to do anything at home.

The nurses were great teachers, but I was still nervous.

Even though Elizabeth qualified for homecare nursing at the time, it was still hard to get homecare nurses to do this work. They rely very heavily on Medicaid reimbursements to pay for the care, and they can make a lot more money working in the hospital. This state of affairs has meant that a lot of the homecare nurses who *are* available are not necessarily the top quality people. Often, they are the ones who couldn't cut it in the hospital.

Not *all* of them, of course. Some of them did this kind of work because they wanted to make their own hours. Some had their own children with special needs and needed a more flexible schedule. There are good apples. But because of some of these structural issues, they tend to be the exception to the rule. Scratch that: in the world of homecare nursing, there *are* no rules. People basically take off whenever they want. They cancel, they show up late all the time or just not at all. But they never get fired.

It's the same with other homecare staff: ABA therapists, home health aides, personal care attendants. Again, they're not *all* bad. There are those who are mission-oriented, who love the work they do and are happy to take these jobs. But, overall, with homecare personnel, you get the lower end of the barrel—the best talent flocks to the institutions, where they get benefits, health insurance, and higher pay rates.

Despite these problems, I was happy to have homecare nurses to help with Elizabeth's central line. But what soon became clear was that I was still the one ultimately responsible for every shift. It's not like families get 24/7 coverage. We could only get the shifts that the nurses were willing to do. So we never got an overnight, for example. All in all, I saw the nursing care more as a backup than a primary source of care.

This lack of quality nursing care is, in fact, one of the reasons I set out later to open up my own nursing agency. But at this point, I was just too busy dealing with Elizabeth and all her complications. With the central line came life-threatening sepsis and infections, of which she had many. It was one thing after another. We were in and out of hospitals *all* the time—and this was when I really started to understand just how difficult our lives were going to be. Chaos had become the new normal. There was a six-month period where Elizabeth was only home from the hospital for maybe two or three weeks in total.

We basically *lived* at Children's, spent many holidays there: Halloween, Thanksgiving, Christmas. Elizabeth was such a fixture that she had her name permanently attached to the window outside her hospital room. She was in Children's Hospital newsletters several times in those early years because she was so beautiful and engaging. It was like a second home for us, and the nurses were amazing, just wonderful. We got really good care. Not just Elizabeth, but me, too. The nurses really *got* me; they understood how difficult it all was for a mom—and treated me like a colleague, not a customer. They would order pizza at night and offer me some. I would sit out at the nurses' station and gossip with them.

They always tried so hard to make life as normal as possible for everyone. I remember one time when we were in the hospital with Elizabeth, it was Halloween, and the nurses and other staff made cute little costumes for all the kids. Each child was dressed as a different colored M&M chocolate, and we all did a trick-or-treat parade through the hospital. Elizabeth was a bright blue M&M.

I also met other moms there who were experiencing the same things I was, and I stayed in touch with many of them. Back then, I was still in the habit of joining pretty much every group out there that needed parent volunteers—focus groups at the hospital, support groups, and more. They all knew to call me because I said "yes" to everything. I did this somewhat out of desperation: you could say I was losing my mind at the time, trying to figure out what was going on with Elizabeth, wrestling to get a diagnosis. But I was also still trying to find my community.

Nobody really knew *why* Elizabeth was sick all the time,

or what exactly was going on with her. At the early inter-vention center, there were other children making some progress in their own ways. This was one of the reasons I knew something was different with Elizabeth. She just wasn't progressing, even gradually. Other kids with CP were being stabilized by therapy and starting to acquire skills. Elizabeth wasn't showing up like a CP kid. It was different. Something was clearly wrong. But nobody could figure it out.

That was when I came across an article in *Exceptional Parent* magazine about mitochondrial disease. I brought it to the doctor and said, "I think Elizabeth has this." The conversation with the pediatrician wasn't the most pleas-ant experience. Frankly, I was surprised by his reaction: this was the doctor I loved, the one who had gotten me involved in the beginning with Massachusetts Families Organizing for Change. But when I showed him the arti-cle, he just looked at me funny, like he didn't trust my instincts—just another crazy patient trying to make sense out of something that couldn't be made sense out of.

A LIFE-CHANGING TRIP

What is mitochondrial disease? Very little was known about it back then. Mitochondria are, of course, struc-tures within our cells. They're the parts of our cells that produce energy. And when they malfunction, it can lead to all sorts of debilitating problems: physical, developmental, and cognitive.

Our doctor in Massachusetts didn't know much about mitochondrial disease and didn't give my theory much credence. He basically said, *no, this is not what Elizabeth has*. But he did agree to some testing and ultimately sent us to a specialist, a doctor down in Atlanta, Dr. Schoffner, who was a leading authority at the time, one of a handful of experts on Mito.

There was no real test for the disease back then—they had only even begun diagnosing it eight years earlier—but some of the results from Elizabeth's exams made it look like she might have some indicators. How could we know for sure? In order to get more information, we had to test specifically for the disease. But you could only do that using genetic material from a fresh muscle, which meant you had to go to where the doctor was.

We went to Atlanta to see Dr. Schoffner. The Ronald McDonald House covered the accommodation, of course, and our flight was paid for by another program. But it required an enormous amount of work on my part, and also my doctor in Massachusetts, to get everything approved. I think it went on for about a month: me trying to get our private insurance and Mass Health to agree to pay for this testing out of state, and out of network. I had to do whatever it took. The hospital in Atlanta wouldn't let us come down until it was guaranteed that they were going to get paid.

So, there were lots of agreements that had to be negotiated, and it took a great deal of advocacy on my part. There were endless phone calls: to our private insurance, to the people at Mass Health, at Children's Hospital in Massachusetts, and the hospital in Atlanta. It seemed like every person I spoke to would point me to somebody else, who then pointed me to somebody else, and so on and so forth.

Side note: if you're working with families who are in crisis like this, make sure you have the right person before you send them on a wild goose chase and have them call ten or twelve more folks. This is why parents give up. If only the professionals would take an extra five minutes to confirm that the person they just sent you to is in fact the right person, we'd all be in a much happier situation.

Luckily, this was during the period of my life when I was becoming better at advocating for my family, learning how to navigate the system and get what we needed. But it was still challenging. There's no one door or one way into the system (more on that to come in chapter 7). It requires a lot of management. I know it took me longer than it needed to because I got frustrated. Even though

I was a better advocate than I used to be, I still yelled at people, which isn't productive. But I was just so desperate for a change, a diagnosis. Something had to be done to help Elizabeth.

We had to wait a few weeks for the results of the diagnosis. And, when we finally got them, it was confusing. We didn't get an exact mitochondrial diagnosis. Instead, Elizabeth's condition closely resembled what is called Leigh's Disease or Leigh syndrome, a rare genetic disorder often characterized by defects of mitochondrial energy production. They gave her a diagnosis of "Leigh's-*like* Disease."

What on earth did that mean? Whatever you called it, I knew it wasn't pretty. It was killing kids. In fact, all of the kids who had been diagnosed with Leigh's had died, because it was such a fast deterioration. And when a kid had been diagnosed really early on, or from birth, the prognosis was even worse. The disease was that much more intense and deadly.

What did this all mean for Elizabeth? That's what I was trying to figure out. Part of me was inspired by the new information: *Now we know what this is. What's next? What are we going to do? How are we going to cure this?* But another part of me fell into a much darker place: for obvious reasons, the diagnosis felt a lot like a death sentence.

For better or worse, it represented an important turning

point in my parent journey. Up until now, I had *suspected* there was an underlying medical condition, not just CP and a seizure disorder. But now I knew for sure that Elizabeth had a degenerative, life-limiting disease.

Dr. Schoffner started her on CoQ10 and Carnitor, and a few other new medicines they were just trying out at the time. We started working with the metabolic and genetic team at Children's Hospital in Boston, which was where the kids with Mito were housed at the time. We also entered Elizabeth into a study being done in Atlanta—hoping that, as they continued to test more samples, the researchers would be able to narrow down exactly what she had.

I wanted to believe Elizabeth could be cured. But the doctor's words didn't give me much hope: "Keep doing what you're doing. You have to treat each symptom as it comes up." In other words, we could treat the seizures, the carnitine deficiency, the respiratory health problems. There were things we could do, he said. But the uncertainty of it all was still very frustrating.

The doctors wouldn't come out and say that Elizabeth had a shortened life expectancy. There was no prognosis on what the outcome would be, no guidance on what her life would look like in the long run. I suppose this approach is better than, for example, the doctor who had made the Swiss cheese comment. But it also just left me with a lot of questions. I looked up Leigh's Disease on the internet, and what I saw there was really scary. Her horrible seizures were not a good sign either, not a good indicator for Elizabeth's future. There were just a lot of things going wrong, it seemed, and I felt in the dark. But this time, it wasn't that the doctors were keeping me in the dark—they just didn't know. The medical understanding of mitochondrial disease was so new, and they didn't have a lot of data.

Where did that leave Elizabeth? Where did it leave me? What was I supposed to do? Part of me wished the doctor had said, "It's cancer, and we're at the stage where we can't do anything else." At least then I would have known it was the end. But with Mito, the diagnosis is so ambiguous. The message is basically: *Yeah, we don't really have anything we can do. We're going to keep treating the symptoms. A lot of kids die, but some don't. We don't know.*

Again, all my usual playbooks were failing me. None of my life skills that had served me so well in the past were going to help me now. It didn't matter that I was smart, driven, a Type A personality. All my checklists and spreadsheets weren't going to get me out of this one. It was then that I started to get quite depressed for a while. I didn't know what to do but wait for Elizabeth's eventual death, terrible as that sounds.

It didn't help that my marriage was falling apart at the same time.

MY BUTTERFLY MOMENT

I'm going to lose Elizabeth. That's what I thought. And somehow, I knew that when Elizabeth died, *if* she died young like that, I would leave Wayne immediately. Is that what I wanted? To leave Wayne? I didn't know. So I just stopped. I pressed pause on life and just cocooned for a while, pulled inward.

I didn't realize it then, but my butterfly moment was the death of so many dreams for me. I had always dreamed of having four or five kids, a big family, a perfect family. I wanted it all: the minivan, the house in the suburbs, the amazing career.

Eventually, I would come out of my cocoon. But it was a long process, a metamorphosis, to come out the other side and into a different way of being. I wasn't a caterpillar anymore, not inching along a tree and eating leaves, but I wasn't yet a butterfly. I knew what I had to do—transform from one kind of creature into another—but I wasn't ready yet. I didn't know what that looked like.

None of that was in the cards. I was in a pretty dark place, but there was one ray of light that stood out. I became aware of a child named Mattie Stepanek who had the same diagnosis as Elizabeth. I saw him on TV. He was only a kid, but he wrote amazing poetry and was championed by everyone from Oprah to Jimmy Carter.

How did I discover Mattie? After receiving Elizabeth's diagnosis of "Leigh's-like Disease" and learning that it was in the muscular dystrophy family, I had reached out to the MD group in our area. They didn't really have anything for her, but I ended up doing some fundraising on their behalf (and got to present a check).

Over the course of these experiences, I read a lot about mitochondrial disease and grew more involved in this world. Mattie was well known and admired in these circles. He was older than Elizabeth—and he was incredible. In his appearances on *Oprah* and his series of *HeartSong* poetry books, he put forth a message of peace that struck a chord around the world.

It felt great to see him on TV. I remember thinking: *Elizabeth's not going to be able to talk like that, but maybe she'll have some gift of her own to give the world*. It was a hopeful moment for me. To my mind, Mattie was an early leader in changing the way the world looks at disability. Back when I was growing up, the special needs kids were usually hidden away, in a classroom in the basement, that sort of thing. We just weren't exposed to them. It's different today—although we still have a very long way to go—and Mattie was instrumental in that, in changing the face of disability. He showed people that disability is *individual.* It runs the gamut from kids like Elizabeth, who can't talk, to those like Mattie, who write bestselling books for goodness' sake. Everyone with special needs is different, and all have their own contributions to make.

Seeing Mattie on TV really changed the way a lot of people thought. I know it changed *my* thinking about what it means to be a successful person. As someone who had always been on the path of career, family, etc., I had believed from a very early age that if I achieved all of those milestones, I would be a successful human being. But when I got to know Elizabeth and see kids like Mattie, I started to realize there's a lot more to being "successful."

Elizabeth was a *very* successful human being: she loved others, she loved God, she worked hard at everything she tried, and she was so present in her life.

Seeing Mattie helped me understand this, and contributed to a real shift in my mindset. I will always remember going with Elizabeth to present our check at the Mattie telethon on TV. Elizabeth just loved being there. She was such a ham—loved having her picture taken, meeting new people, loved all the phones ringing and the bustling activity.

Thank God that Mattie's family were brave enough to share him with the world. It's not an easy thing to open yourself and your family up in that way. But it's all worth it, if it can help others, as I would later learn. For now, I was still in my cocoon.

ALLOWING YOURSELF TO GRIEVE

Different parents have different reactions to receiving a diagnosis for their child. I went inward and even fell into a bit of a depression. For many parents, there is a grieving that takes place. It is indeed a kind of loss, and we honor that loss by grieving for the child we thought we would have, the life we thought we'd have, the dream of how things could have been.

There's no one right way to deal with the fallout of a diagnosis or to process the new information. What's important is that you *allow* yourself to go through whatever emotions you're feeling, to experience them in full. In other words, you can't go *around* your emotions—your sadness, your anger, your grief. You can only go *through* them. The information and processing is not linear. It's not "one step at a time," "one foot in front of the other," like people say.

I always imagined the process of healing more as being like ocean waves crashing over me. I grew up going to the beach all summer long in East Boston, so I have a connection to the sea. I remember standing in front of the powerful waves and feeling them coming at me and knocking me over. I'd try to get up and take a step but then another wave would come. Sometimes the waves would come in wildly different intervals. Sometimes they'd come from different directions.

That's what it felt like, at the time, with my grief and my processing. A total storm at sea. I wasn't thinking straight. I had really compartmentalized. Half of me was in army general mode, strategizing, figuring everything out, finding our way down to Atlanta, finding a great PT and OT, doing everything I could to give Elizabeth the best life possible. But then another side of me was a *mess*. The two sides weren't reconciled to each other. It was like being Dr. Jekyll and Mr. Hyde. And I definitely wasn't good at hiding the mess inside. It was all over the place, oozing out in weird, unexpected ways.

For example, one of my reactions to Elizabeth's mitochondrial diagnosis was—readers, get ready for this—to have another baby with Wayne. I know how crazy that must sound. The only way I can explain it is that I wanted and needed a do-over. To this day, I feel guilty saying that: like a slap in the face to Elizabeth. But it's the truth. And if I'm being really raw and honest, it was even deeper: I still wanted my "perfect baby" and my perfect mommy experience, selfish as that may sound.

I wanted to hear my child call me "Mommy." I wanted it so bad. I wanted to watch first steps. With Elizabeth, I had missed all of those opportunities, and I craved them. I wanted to raise a little me, somebody who was going to be smart and go to college and have a great career and bring me grandkids and all of those things. Somebody who wasn't going to die on me.

I knew in my gut that my marriage was not going to last, so my thinking was: *alright, Annie, this is your last chance.* Maybe I was grasping at straws. All that mattered to me was having that do-over opportunity. Before long, I was pregnant, and I became very caught-up in trying to have a healthy pregnancy and a healthy baby. It wasn't easy. Picture me at nine months, ready to pop, and still running back and forth to the hospital with Elizabeth, pulling her wheelchair in and out of the car. I was still bringing her to school every day, forty-five minutes away in traffic, because I couldn't bear to put my fragile baby on a bus with strangers.

Caroline was born on December 4th, 2000. I had to have another C-section because my first was an emergency, and it was dangerous to try to deliver naturally. But the doctor this time was really amazing, as was his whole team. The experience couldn't have been more different than after I had given birth to Elizabeth four-and-a-half years earlier and had felt so in the dark. At Brigham Women's Hospital in Boston, a high-risk OBGYN talked me through it all, explaining what was happening every step of the way. The doctor really understood my anxiety. I was not unique to him. Most of his patients had been through similar experiences.

I even had my own room at the Brigham. It was like staying in a fancy hotel. I got to order from a menu for all my meals. Got to cuddle with Caroline, nurse her, all the stuff I never had a chance to do with Elizabeth.

Having a healthy pregnancy, a healthy birth, and a child who met all of her developmental milestones was a really good thing for me. There's no other way of saying it: Caroline healed me. She was my big do-over. It was indeed just what I needed.

But, while I was on a path to healing, Wayne was headed in the other direction.

CHAPTER FOUR

The Death of a Marriage

In 2001, after telling Wayne that I wanted a divorce, he moved out of the house and got his own apartment in town—but not before emptying our joint bank account, meager as it was, to pay for the rent and security deposit on his new place. Meanwhile, my utilities got shut off because I had no money left to pay the bills. I was left with a baby and a very sick, disabled five-year-old. I needed to get a job right away.

I'll never really understand what Wayne was going through at that time, but I didn't have the energy to be understanding and caring towards him. He left me in a very difficult situation.

He was going downhill fast. Soon, I discovered he was suffering not just from depression but a host of other mental health issues. It spiraled out of control very quickly. He was only in his new apartment for eight or nine months. A while later, he needed to be hospitalized. I thought he was going to kill himself. So did his brother and cousin. They came up from Virginia and got him.

Was I sad? Was I concerned about him and his health? Yes and yes, but there was nothing I could do for him at that point. I was only one human being, and my hands were so full already: not only did I have the new baby, but Elizabeth was still really sick. We had been feeding her via TPN (total parenteral nutrition), a method where there is no actual eating or digestion. Rather, fluids containing nutrients go directly into a vein.

Eventually, I decided to stop the TPN and just keep trying to feed her through her gut. The doctors weren't happy about it. They even told me there was a chance she would die. We had something called an ethics review committee meeting, where we discussed the pros and cons.

I explained my reasoning: it was a quality-of-life thing. With the TPN, she was always getting infected; she was spending more time in the hospital than she was at home. And it was keeping her from some of the few activities in life that gave her real pleasure, like going in the pool. It was also a struggle to go to school with the TPN. She needed a nurse with her around the clock, and the nurse had to have special skills and training to deal with her central line and other issues.

The ethics meeting was not easy. It was definitely an intimidating environment to be in. On one side of the table sat a whole slew of professionals from the hospital. On the other, there was just me. And Wayne. I didn't really understand what I was getting into until I was actually in the room. It was like walking into the lion's den. I didn't realize they could call in the DCF (Department of Children and Families) or go to court if they felt I wasn't making the right decision for Elizabeth. It happens a lot there.

Thankfully, in my case, they agreed to let us try my plan. I think what made the difference was they could see I had done a ton of research, and it wasn't just an impulsive decision. I had talked to my priest, read lots of articles, and more.

Overall, the people in the meeting were folks from Children's who I knew and had a good relationship with. But I think they were worried that I was just doing this because I was tired—tired of being in the hospital, tired of doing the central line. That wasn't the case, but if it were, their response would have probably been very different. They would have said, "Well, if the child needs it, we're going to do it, whether you can provide it or not." But because I had done my homework, it disarmed them. They gave me the benefit of the doubt. All in all, it was a victory. And it did make a difference to Elizabeth's quality of life. But it was still a very tough time for her—and for the rest of us.

Family-wise, I think what it came down to, both with Elizabeth and my marriage, was a realization that everything is a give and take, there's no solution that fixes all. A family is made up of many people, all of whose needs are important. You can't sacrifice it all for one member of the family, and you can't give your time and energy in one direction without pulling back from somewhere else.

In terms of marriage, it was clear as day to me that my kids took priority over my husband. I was already taking care of Elizabeth and Caroline. I couldn't spend any energy taking care of Wayne as well. I simply wasn't strong enough. And God help me, but I have to be honest: I really didn't *want* to care of Wayne. I didn't feel the love anymore, and I didn't feel like it was my duty. As a practicing Catholic, I didn't take the end of a marriage lightly. I was really torn. After all, I had made a vow in church: for sicker or poorer, for better or worse. This was definitely "worse"—but I just couldn't do it.

I certainly never thought of myself as someone who would get divorced, but one can only try for so long. In fact, earlier that fall, we had gone on a family vacation:

not just me and Wayne and kids, but also my mom, my sister and her kids, and my brother and his kids. We all went down to Florida, to Universal Studios Orlando.

Our intention was to have a nice time together in "the happiest place on Earth," but Wayne and I ended up having such a bad fight that the hotel security called to see what was going on. It was so serious that they were going to have come up to the room. I don't even remember what the fight was about, but Wayne was freaking out and just couldn't calm down.

At the time, I remember thinking: *oh yeah, this marriage is dead, there's nothing here.*

But then, right when we got back to Massachusetts, 9/11 happened. The tragedy actually brought us together, for a minute at least, because Wayne was traveling at the time for business, in New York—and when the towers fell, I didn't know where he was and couldn't get ahold of him. I was really scared. I couldn't get through to him all day. Finally, he called: he was safe in New Jersey, waiting to get home.

For a brief moment, I imagined I had gotten a different call, with news that he had died in the horrific events. I thought to myself, *well this is what it would be like to not have a husband,* and it made me appreciate him. But that feeling didn't last long. A couple months later, he was out of the house.

I knew how badly he was suffering psychologically, knew he was depressed and worse, but honestly, I just didn't care anymore. There was only so much care to go around. I had to put myself and my kids first. It was a terrible choice to make, like a "Sophie's choice," but the answer was clear. Wayne was a grown-up. Yes, he was mentally ill, and I am sympathetic to anyone who suffers from a disease. But let me not beat around the bush: he also wasn't very good to me. It wasn't like he was depressed but grateful. He could be mean and rotten.

Things even got physical once. It happened right before he left. I had just told him I wanted the divorce, and instead of talking it through and coming up with a plan, he just decided to leave then and there. But not before we had a scuffle. To be clear, I didn't tell him to leave; he did that on his own. I didn't yell or throw him out. That wasn't my intention whatsoever. He is the father of my kids and that meant a lot to me. My goal was simply to tell him what I wanted and work out the details like grown-ups. (To this day, he maintains that I threw him out. Like many divorced couples, we don't see eye-to-eye on the details.)

I didn't take any of this lightly. But it was far too late to fix things now. We had tried marriage counseling before, but it was useless—he just made it all about him. It didn't help, either, that our therapist had no clue whatsoever what it's like to raise a sick child. Her advice about going on dates nights, etc., might have been okay for your average parents, but was woefully mismatched to the unique circumstances of our family situation.

That's the thing about being a special needs parent: it's like you're living in a different reality, and other people are speaking a foreign language. Date night? We would have needed a nurse to take care of Elizabeth *plus* another person to watch Caroline. I couldn't get enough nursing hours as it was. There was a constant shortage of nurses to take care of Elizabeth. I was already struggling just to get the bare minimum of help I needed.

Then, there were, of course, the financial considerations. I had no savings. After Wayne left, there was no choice but for me to go get a job and start making money. I didn't get any financial support from Wayne for about two years after he left. My mom, who had lived with us since before Caroline was born, helped me to make ends meet. She was still working at the time and helped me pay the bills. She's the only reason I survived during that timeframe when I was trying to get steady employment and make money.

Without her help, I don't know what I would have done.

I wouldn't have been able to keep the house or take care of my children. I probably would've ended up in public housing. But because of her, I was able to cobble together a new job for myself that would allow me to work within the parameters of my crazy life and parenting situation.

MY NURSING AGENCY

A year or two earlier, I had started my own nursing agency. At the time, it wasn't intended to be a "*job* job," but after Wayne left, I ended up transforming it, out of necessity, into a full-time gig—but one where I could take baby Caroline with me or work from home sometimes.

The nursing agency had been born out of my frustration with homecare nursing, my personal experiences with nurses who cancelled, or didn't show up, or worse. I still remember one time when I was about to give birth to Caroline. I was trying to find enough care for Elizabeth, who still had her central line in. I knew I was going to have to go to the hospital soon to give birth to Caroline and would need solid coverage for Elizabeth. Wayne wanted to be at the hospital with me, and he didn't really know how to do any of the more complicated homecare stuff anyway. My mom didn't either. She was a great caregiver but never learned to be the nurse. So I knew I had to get everything in place, with all the best people, in advance. I couldn't have somebody call out sick.

Normally, what happened when a nurse called sick was that I became the backup plan. But I was going to be in the hospital having my baby. I couldn't be the backup plan. What was I going to do? If I didn't have a nurse for Elizabeth, she would wind up in the hospital, too.

One nurse wanted me to pay her double to do extra shifts. I mean, not just pay for the extra shifts but pay twice the normal rate each time she came. It was totally against the rules. What she was proposing was actually Medicaid fraud. So I called her nursing agency and complained, but they refused to do anything. They knew I was right. But they argued that if they fired the nurse, it would just mean I would be left with no coverage. Their attitude was that something was better than nothing.

But something is *not* always better than nothing when you're talking about, for example, a nurse dropping a sterile syringe on the floor and then picking it up and using it. That almost happened to us. I saw it fall on the floor, and the nurse was about to put it to Elizabeth's central line. Luckily, I stopped her just in time. It made me shudder to think about what I had missed when I was maybe napping or taking care of Caroline, or when Elizabeth was at school. As a parent, you had to find a way to trust people, but the system was not designed to instill confidence.

So, to say that families should just take what they can

get is really not acceptable. It makes people feel like they're second-class citizens and not entitled to good, proper care. It was one of the reasons I started my own agency. I was just fed up with how unscrupulous some of these folks were. They take advantage because they know parents like me are desperate for help. Some nurses will demand extra pay under the table. And they *get* it, because the families are vulnerable and have no other options, and because the nurses know their jobs are safe and the agencies are not going to discipline them.

With my nursing agency, I set out to change all that, at least in part. It was a real mission for me. I wasn't out to make money with it, but after Wayne left, I had to. And even that wasn't enough: the revenue was up and down, with no benefits, no real security. We really had to take care of the nurses first so that they would take care of the kids.

Luckily, I had a friend who offered me a job around that time as a consultant at a CPA firm. I worked there for a while, and it helped me get financially stable. But eventually, the constraints of my family life just made it impossible to continue. All along, what I really wanted was to be an attorney. But that would have to wait. It just wasn't possible in my situation at that time.

Luckily, at a certain point after Wayne's mental break-down, he started to come back to reality and get his act together. He was working for his family in Virginia, where he had a ready-made job waiting for him. So he was doing okay, making a living again, after having lost his job in Massachusetts.

For a split second, I actually considered moving back to Virginia, not to get back together with him, but just to make life easier. I didn't think I could make it in Natick on my own. Honestly, I just didn't have enough money. It was too hard to work and take care of the kids. Plus, Elizabeth's situation was so dicey. There were constant medical issues coming up. I just felt so scared all the time. It was so hard to work and take care of the kids. I want to be able to say I felt strong and independent at the time. There was still that side of me, the army general. But inside, I didn't feel pow-erful. I wasn't up to the challenge—and that's why I even considered, however briefly, the possibility of moving back.

The idea was that I'd move down with Elizabeth and Caroline, and Wayne would stay with his parents in Vir-ginia—and help to pay the rent for me and the kids to live somewhere nearby. Eventually, we'd sell the house in Natick and buy a nicer house in VA for the kids and me.

It was a bad idea, and it degenerated quickly. The conversation didn't really go anywhere, and deep down I knew it was just my desperation talking. After all that I had gone through, uprooting ourselves to come to Boston to get better care for Elizabeth, was I really considering going back? No. I knew it was a mistake, so I never pulled the trigger. Eventually, we finalized our divorce, and that was that. But it took almost three years from beginning to end for us to make it official. Initially, he wasn't in any kind of stable frame of mind where he could deal with it, so I just kind of waited. It was also important to me that we did it right.

While he was still in his apartment in Natick, he would come and visit the kids multiple times a week. There wasn't really any choice but to do it there, because of how hard it was for Elizabeth to go anywhere in her wheel-chair. She was very fragile—but also Wayne didn't know how to do most of her care. He never learned. I'm not sure if this was on purpose or if he just wasn't capable. I never really got to the bottom of that. But the fact of the matter was he just didn't know how to prepare her med-ications and do all the stuff he needed to do. I had pages and pages of med lists and instructions posted up on our cabinet. But Wayne just wasn't reliable: he couldn't follow directions or remember the process.

On a personal level, he and I didn't talk much when we saw each other, but we didn't really fight either. It had gotten kind of quiet at that point, but he was acting increasingly crazy, talking about gypsies coming to steal the kids and other bizarre theories. He had always been weird, but not like this. It wasn't until after he left the house that he descended into madness. Looking back now, I realize he had a lot of issues I didn't know about when I married him—he is a very fragile person—and having Elizabeth was what broke him. He's never been the same since.

For me, however, the more I saw him wigging out in the weeks and months after he left the house, the more I *knew* I had made the right decision. The kids didn't need to witness his self-destruction. I let him see them, of course—I never questioned the importance of them having a relationship with their father—but it was always on my terms. At the house. It doesn't surprise me that he never challenged me on that, or asked if he could take them overnight. I think he knew he wasn't safe.

Through the years, even after we were divorced, I continued to work hard to make sure the kids had a relationship with him. I fed him and let him sleep over at the house when he visited. I made it easy for him to see his kids as often as he wanted. I let him come for pretty much every holiday: Christmas, Valentine's Day, Easter, Thanksgiving, and birthdays. It wasn't fun for me—he acted like it was still his house, and I had to basically cater to him while he was there—but I did it for the kids. It was a sacrifice I was willing to make.

I even trooped the kids down to Virginia and North Carolina to see him and his family so that the kids could have a relationship with their cousins and their grandparents. It was not easy, with Elizabeth so sick. The drive there and back was twelve hours. Imagine being in the car for that long with two little kids, one in a wheelchair. Of course, even at this age Elizabeth wore diapers, but now she was too big to get changed easily in the bathroom. I couldn't use the baby-changing stations anymore. And she couldn't stand up or sit on a toilet. So on these long drives, we'd have to pull into rest stops and change her wet stools with her leaning on me while I wiped her bottom. And that was just the diapers. I also had to hook up her G-tube for feeding, give her meds, and more. It was nearly impossible.

These are the kinds of challenges that don't even cross the minds of families with typically-developing kids. Travel is a different experience entirely when you have a disabled child. You can't just pack up for an overnight when you have to pack heavy bags of medical equipment or an oxygen tank or whatever the case may be.

Families do it, but it's so hard. When this is your reality as a parent, it can almost stunt you as a person. It's like you're stuck in a relationship that doesn't work. Add divorce to the mix and it's even more complicated. There are so many families out there who twist themselves into crazy positions and arrangements to make it work for the kids. The mom might live upstairs while the dad lives downstairs. Or they'll take turns, and one will live at the house for a week and then switch.

It's not easy, but we do it for our kids. That's how it was for me, and it still is. I knew I was making the right decisions, doing the right thing for Elizabeth and Caroline, by taking them on those trips down to Virginia and North Carolina. Wayne's parents also greatly appreciated it. They were not very mobile themselves, so it allowed them to see their grandchildren much more often than would have been possible otherwise. They told me how grateful they were, and so did Wayne. To hear them say that and express their appreciation— and to hear Caroline talk about her cousins and the beagles at Grandma and Grandpa's house—made it all worthwhile.

Growing up, my girls loved their dad, and there are so many great memories of the fun times they had together. Even though it was hard after Wayne left, it was better. I never looked back at the separation or divorce and doubted my decision, not even once. It was absolutely the best parenting decision I could have made for my kids.

When our divorce was finalized in 2003, it was almost anticlimactic. We went to court together, were in and out in five minutes, and that was that—I was divorced. Wayne and I drove to the proceedings together, in the same car, and left together.

I suppose it was a good thing that it all went so smoothly. I had a lawyer friend write up an agreement for us, but Wayne never got a lawyer, and we never went back and forth like so many couples do. We figured it all out, and I'm proud of how we did it. We just kind of worked it out amongst ourselves, which probably saved us a lot of time and money.

But there was also something bizarre and kind of sad about how easy it was. A marriage opens with a big to-do but ends with a whimper. I thought back to our wedding and everything that went into it—the church, the big reception, all the planning—but then when it came to the divorce, it was like I snapped my finger, signed a piece of paper, and it was all over.

Not that I regretted it whatsoever. It was absolutely what I wanted. I was doing okay on my own. I was working. My mom was helping. And then, soon after the divorce, my mom retired so that she could be home with the kids, which allowed me to be at work during the day.

Not everyone has that luxury, of course. And even among those who do have the option of leaning on family members for help, many feel hesitant to ask. They don't want to be a burden.

A CRY FOR HELP

No doubt about it: it's *much* easier to care for a sick or disabled child when you have help from family. Unfortunately, many parents just don't have anyone like that nearby. It can make life very difficult for them. It takes a village, as the saying goes. But when you're raising a special needs child and you need that help and support more than ever, sometimes there are just no villagers around!

Sounds like such an easy, straightforward principle—*it takes a village*—doesn't it? But not with a kid like Elizabeth. It's one thing to keep an eye and make sure your neighbor's child doesn't chase a ball into the street. But to, say, change a nine-year-old's diaper is something else entirely, even for the child's own grandparents. There are a number of tasks that can be really scary and difficult. You have to be physically able to transfer a child from a wheelchair to a bed, or to deal with a seizure. There is so much involved, and for kids like Elizabeth, so much equipment. It's not like you can just schlep that stuff to somebody else's house.

Of course, many extended families *do* participate in a big

way. And many parents of special needs children end up either moving in with their parents or having their parents move in with them, like my mom did with me and Wayne.

It is also, sadly, very common for parents of special needs children to get divorced. Divorce is never easy, but it can be especially hard on these families. Not only financially, although that's certainly a big part of it, but also in terms of logistics. Special needs kids often have trouble with transitions and don't go back and forth between households very well.

There's no sugarcoating it: divorce can be pretty crappy. I'm just grateful that we made it work, that we never had to hire attorneys to battle out it with each other, and never had to go back to court in the years since. It hasn't always been easy. Of course, there was bickering, but we both loved the kids, and that guided us over the years.

When you keep the focus on the kids and what's good for them, rather than on what one parent may want in this or that situation, it makes all the difference. It can really save you and keep things from getting ugly, during and after a divorce.

For all those who are still happily married, please understand: having a special needs child doesn't have to be a death sentence for a marriage. In my case, there was lot more going on with Wayne, my feelings for him, and his unraveling mental health. It was an already volatile situation, and the parenting challenges just amplified it. Other couples might do better in couples counseling than we did. The key is to look for specialists who have experience with special needs families and understand the unique stresses.

Above all, be easy on yourselves: accept that life is never going to be like it once was, and that's okay. Give yourself, and your husband or your wife, a pat on the back for having made it this far.

In my case, there was no saving the marriage. But once I was honest with myself about how my life had changed, once I started to let that past roll away, it was like a weight had been lifted. Yes, I was going to have to let go of some of my long-held hopes and dreams, but there was a way to do it without sadness or regret. Moreover, there was an opportunity to create exciting new goals that reflected the new person I was becoming.

CHAPTER FIVE

My So-Called Career

Ever since Elizabeth was born, I had put almost all of my professional ambitions on hold. What choice did I have? As almost all parents who have been on this special needs journey will attest, it is virtually impossible to avoid some sort of rupture in your work life along the way.

On the brighter side, parents often come out of it with a greater self-awareness and sense of purpose. This was certainly true in my case. My experience with Elizabeth was directly responsible for putting me on a new path. It led to my interest in civil-rights law and, ultimately, to becoming an attorney specializing in disability civil rights and long-term care planning.

As hard as it was at times—and make no mistake, trying to balance work and career with the demands of parenting a special needs child *will* often feel insurmountable—I grew to love my life in all of its facets. I loved what I ended up doing, loved the people I got to help and the people who've helped me.

Working in this area of special needs law is wonderfully collaborative. Even when it's sad, it's honest and raw in the best possible way. It's deeply personal and life sustaining. It nourished me when I needed it most. How many people can say that they love going to work every day? I am so lucky and grateful to Elizabeth for having given me this gift. Because of her, I was introduced to many, many wonderful people.

But of course, none of this happened overnight, and when I first set out to pursue a law career, I couldn't even get an interview.

TRYING TO CATCH A BREAK

I had always wanted to be a lawyer, and had passed the bar on my first try after finishing law school at Howard University in DC.

Howard is an HBCU, which stands for "Historically Black Colleges and Universities," but there are some white students there as well. I had gotten into five different law schools, and they all offered scholarships. But Howard was the only one that gave me a full ride, which was obviously important to someone like me who was paying their own way through school.

I also really wanted to be in DC. I can't say exactly why. It just felt like a place where I could do important things. At the time, I didn't know *what* I wanted to do. But I had a lot of drive and ambition in those days; I felt like I was destined for something big—and Washington just seemed like the right location to chase my dreams. That, and of course, Howard Law School was itself a highly respected institution. It's also where I met Wayne; he was a law student there at the same time. We graduated together and then moved to Virginia that same year to get married.

That's when I became pregnant with Elizabeth. It happened right away. Catholic birth control, as they say.

Then, after Elizabeth was born, unsurprisingly my career plans came to a halt. I had to postpone taking the bar. In fact, it wasn't until we moved to Boston that I signed up for the exam and took a bar review class. Not one of those fancy prep courses. I definitely couldn't afford that. It was just a bare-bones, one-week thing.

It wasn't easy to find time to go to the review class while still taking care of Elizabeth. This was when she was still very young, not in school yet. I was lucky to have some help from my mom. She had a full-time job herself at the time, but she lent a hand as best she could. She'd watch the baby at night so I could go to the review class. But then when it came to the actual studying for the bar, that was even harder. I would stay up, buried in my books, through the night, all night. Then I'd be up with the baby all day. I was exhausted.

These are the kinds of situations that parents of typically developing kids just don't understand. I hear it all the time: "Well, what about putting her in daycare?" No, there *is* no daycare for special needs kids. There's no place to go for a kid like Elizabeth who has seizures and health issues and developmental issues and needs a one-to-one. I tried. I went to so many places to see if they would take her, even just for a few hours. Nobody would. They all said they weren't equipped to handle her. The only option for me and other parents in this situation is private nannies, and who can afford that?

I remember thinking, why hadn't anybody figured out a solution to this? It didn't seem like such a big problem. Why wasn't there any place to go? Why wouldn't the government want to solve this issue? It sounded to me like a win-win: not only would it help the parents, but it would allow them to work, be more productive, pay more taxes, contribute more to the economy.

I finally found a respite center in Hopkinton that was able

to take Elizabeth. It was an amazing place that had been started by a mom of a special needs son who had passed away. The center had a great infant/toddler playgroup, and best of all, it was inexpensive. They took the kids a couple of mornings a week, depending on what you needed. What a blessing it was for me. It gave me the opportunity to do a little bit of work on the side and get started on my career. All thanks to a mom who had been resourceful enough to recognize a problem and figure out a solution. It wasn't perfect: it wasn't daycare five days a week, eight hours a day. But it was a big help.

For one thing, it allowed me to actually rest once in a while. This was during a period when Elizabeth was up most nights, multiple times. Medically, it was very busy. She was sick a lot: there was always something or other going on health-wise with her. So to be able to just get away from it for an hour, to put the seat of my car back and take a nap there, was incredible. Or I would go to a café and have a cup of tea and a muffin. It sounds like no big deal, but to be able to just sit in peace and have thoughts that weren't completely overtaken by Elizabeth's care was huge for me.

Studies show that caring for a child with medical issues or disabilities can be life limiting and physically disastrous for the parents. I know I've had more than my share of injuries. I had arthritis in my hand and had to have surgery where they removed a bone and restructured my whole hand. I've had back problems, knee problems. I've slipped and fallen while trying to transfer Elizabeth from her wheelchair.

And that's nothing compared to the psychological damage of living with PTSD (post-traumatic stress disorder), as so many of us do, being in and out of the hospital, not being able to eat and sleep well. Parents of kids with special needs tend to be heavier than average. We are more prone to diabetes, high blood pressure, heart disease, and all kinds of ailments. We're just so impacted by the constant caregiving.

Having some kind of respite—a village of one form or another to lend a hand—can help lift some of those layers of pain and stress that accumulate over the years for us parents. And it just makes all the sense in the world for us as society to put resources into supporting families in these situations. To do otherwise is tremendously costly: not only in the sense that we can't be as productive—can't work and make income and revenue to contribute to the economy—but also, we end up being heavy users of the medical system ourselves.

Once Elizabeth was of school age, more options opened up to me, thank God. At the age of three, she started qualifying for home nursing. And once she had a one-to-one nurse with her, I was able to do a lot more work, because she was safe at home with the nurse.

It was at that time that I started my nursing agency. My thinking was that it would be a great way to help families like mine. As readers will remember from the previous chapter, I had seen firsthand just how broken the system actually was. I had an almost pathological need to fix things. My agency was born out of that impulse to fix the nursing system. But as a solution, ours was limited in scope. The agency was only for kids with critical healthcare needs. It wasn't available to kids with autism or intellectual disabilities, who didn't have any healthcare interventions that required a nurse.

Still, the nursing agency was good for the families it helped. And it was good for me in that I was able to create a job for myself. For a while, I had two tracks going on. I had the agency, which was awesome and fun. It was serving a purpose, but also I could bring my kids to work, work from home, do whatever I needed.

Then, at the same time, I was still trying, little by little, to pursue my law career. When it came down to it, I didn't *want* to be running a nursing agency. I did that out of necessity because I couldn't get good nurses for my own family, and I just knew there was a better way. I'm glad I did. The agency was successful, and a year and a half in, I was able to merge it with a nonprofit that another mom had started. I'm really proud of how that turned out. Even though it's still hard to find homecare nurses, pediatric home care in general is a lot better now than it used to be—and I believe we played a small part in that by challenging the status quo and what was considered acceptable care at the time.

Because of the nursing agency, I was highlighted in an article in the *Wall Street Journal*, along with a couple of other parents around the country, on special needs moms and dads who were creating their own careers or their own companies that weren't only serving themselves but also the community. It was very cool to be recognized in that way. But I wanted to do more.

All along, I was paving the way for the law thing. After Caroline was born in 2000, I started to look into MBA programs. In 2002, I started at Suffolk University in Boston, and got my business degree there in 2004. I began to take law cases, but had to be careful about only taking on responsibilities that I could actually handle, given my family situation. For example, in those early days, I never took any court work. I just couldn't. I couldn't commit to being reliable in that way. What if Elizabeth needed me? There was always some emergency that could come up. And when you're doing court work, that's not good enough.

So I did other kinds of work instead. I launched into a lot of advocacy, estate planning, special needs trusts. These were all important responsibilities, but they didn't require being in court and didn't have serious deadlines. Plus, I was working with families who were in similar situations as I was with Elizabeth, and so they tended to be understanding. Unlike in the corporate world, I could say to these clients, "Let's meet at 6:00 p.m."—it was good for them, and it was good for me, because my mom could watch the baby.

It felt great to finally be practicing law. I even got a tiny, one-room office, in the center of my town, Natick. It wasn't much, but I had a phone there and a desk. It was a space of my own.

There was a steep learning curve. I didn't have anybody to review my work. At law school, they don't teach you anything about business, about running your own law practice. They only teach you the law, not the hands-on practical stuff. None of it was easy, but I got there. I couldn't have done it without the help of two great mentors.

THE IMPORTANCE OF MENTORSHIP

I became close, during this period of my life, with two other special needs moms, both of whom were lawyers themselves. They had also both started their own practices. Theresa (Teri) Varnet was probably fifteen years ahead of me, and Barbara Jackins was ten years ahead. They were both already very well-established.

I got connected with them just by picking up the phone and calling. They had both been recommended to me by other parents. You remember Susan Nadworny? She told me about them. I also heard about Teri from the folks at the respite center. She and Barbara both seemed so impressive. I wanted to know how they did it.

Teri and Barbara couldn't have been nicer. They were so generous in answering my questions. Not only that, but Teri gave me some cases early on, and also had me work with her a bit here and there. As for Barbara, she graciously reviewed my work for me from time to time. Through the years, she has been an amazing backup person for me when things have come up and I couldn't get to court. We even shared an office for a few years in our careers.

Both ladies have been wonderful friends, and I owe them a lot. I know I couldn't have gotten any traction in those early days if it weren't for their help and support. They were my network. And it's so important, as a special needs parent, to have a network like this to keep you on your career path. Or sometimes even to give you work.

That was definitely the case for me before my practice

really got off the ground. I was doing legal work, but it wasn't enough to pay the bills. So one of my friends gave me a job as a business consultant in a CPA firm. The work itself was not interesting to me, but it was a paycheck. After I got divorced, I needed a solid income. The nursing agency stuff wasn't cutting it. That was more of an entrepreneurial income: when there was money coming in, I gave myself a little paycheck. But it wasn't consistent or reliable. And, of course, there were no benefits.

Maybe, above all, the problem for me with the nursing agency work was that it was too close to home emotionally, seeing all those sick kids. In a very short period of time, about two years, I had seen two of our patients pass away. They were both only three years old. It was too difficult for me to deal with, too painful. And I'm not a clinical person. But as creator of the nursing agency, the person who had recruited these families, I had to be right there with the nurses—not giving medical care myself, obviously, but definitely being part of the team that took care of these kids and their parents.

I went to a lot of funerals in those early years. Not just the kids I knew through the nursing agency but also the ones through early intervention, school, and more. It was really hard to go to those funerals. If you've ever been to the funeral of a child, with all of its pain and surrealism, you will understand. It didn't help that I still had it in the back of my mind that Elizabeth's diagnosis was a death sentence. I didn't like being reminded of that, but it was impossible to escape, especially when I was running my own nursing agency. So the opportunity at the CPA firm came along at just the right time, and Sarah was a great friend to take a chance on me. The business consultant position there was my first real "*job* job." And through that employer, I got great health insurance, for my kids and myself. Not a negligible matter when you're talking about someone with as many medical problems as Elizabeth!

And it's not like anyone else was going to hire me. I tried, but in an employer's eyes, I was pretty much a train wreck. I had been out of the workforce for so long, and I hadn't taken the traditional path coming out of law school. Now, I couldn't commit to a full-time schedule. I couldn't really at the CPA firm, either, but somehow I fudged it. I had to.

MANAGING HOME AND WORK

It's hard to understand these dilemmas if you've never been in the situation, having to look for a job as a special needs parent. People ask me about it a lot. "How does the employer even know that you have a disabled child?" they ask. "How do they know you're a single parent?" Well, they know because it comes up, in the context of having to ask them about flexibility. The minute it comes up, they know what your issues are. And keep in mind: you are *not* a protected class. Employers can and do discriminate if they think you're going to be absent all the time because you can't manage your home life and work life.

So it's really not something you can hide. Not to mention that, in my case, I was already starting to develop a small reputation in legal circles. People already kind of knew who I was. I had been putting myself out there and volunteering for so many things. I already knew I wanted to do disability law, special needs law, so I talked a lot about it— talked about my passion, how I got into this work, why I was doing what I was doing. Even when I was interviewing for the CPA job, it's not like I could really skirt the issue.

Luckily, it worked out. The CPA job saved me. Without it, I might have lost the house. And if that had happened, it would have been really hard to maintain Elizabeth's quality of care.

I did the CPA thing for almost a year and a half, and it sustained me during that tough time. Eventually, the job moved from Natick to Boston, and I couldn't go to Boston every day. I did for a while, but it was unsustainable. There was so much traffic, and it made me nervous to be so far away from Elizabeth. What if there was an emergency? Plus, the parking was forty dollars a day, which was eating up a huge amount of my paycheck.

Ultimately, I had to let that job go. But I'll always be grateful to my friend who helped me out in a difficult time and got me in there. She was generous and kind all around: whenever I had to take time off, she was there.

It was a sidetrack, in terms of my career, but it was necessary for survival. Meanwhile, I was plotting out my long-term plan.

STEP BY STEP

Through those early years of the nursing agency, then the consulting job, and taking on legal cases little by little, I was laying the foundation to make the next move. How was I going to get there?

First thing I did was join a lot of groups. I volunteered, sat on boards, participated in focus groups. Every time somebody needed a volunteer for a project, I jumped on it. I did volunteer work at Children's Hospital, at the local ARC (Association for Retarded Citizens), at Easter Seals, in the school district. Anything and everything I could think of. I even started a support group myself, but it never really gained momentum.

All the while, I was sowing the seeds of developing a real law practice and getting my name out there. I knew that in order for me to be successful, I had to build my reputation. People had to know who I was. That's how they would come to me later when I was able to really get my practice up and running, around 2004.

That was always the plan in the back of my mind. I would tell myself, *people are going to know who Annette Hines is.* I wanted them to think of me and make the connection that I was a lawyer, an advocate, and a mom. Then, by the time I was ready to do this work on a full scale, I would have a huge network of connections. And that's exactly what happened. It was the key to my success. I had my eye on the long haul. I never stopped thinking about the future. But I also did what I had to do short term to take care of my kids.

Eventually, I got hired by a couple different law firms. By this point, I had run my own practice for about five years and had built a name for myself. But I was looking to join another practice with the clients I already had. I wanted the security of being part of a larger firm. I had always wanted that. It was too hard to be a lawyer and a parent to Elizabeth and Caroline *and* run a business at the same time. But it's not like I could have just applied and gotten hired when I was younger. I had to build what we call a portable practice and make myself attractive to a firm.

Now I had that. I had a client list and income. So I joined a firm of counsel, which means that I was a contract employee. But I was able to get benefits, which was really helpful. I hadn't had such good health insurance since the CPA firm. I worked at that law practice for two years, and they were pretty understanding about me and my situation. But I knew I was never going to be a partner there. The special needs aspect of the practice wasn't as important to them as it was to me. It was more of a side note.

But then, I got recruited by another firm that had a significant special needs focus. I thought it was going to be great, but I only lasted eight months there. I was the proverbial square peg in the round hole. No matter how much money I made or how many clients I brought into the firm, I never really fit in. My family situation made it impossible for me to attend all the law firm events, or to work late or on the weekends. And even though they cared about special needs law, they still couldn't wrap their heads around a different way of working. It was their loss, because I was still producing a lot of revenue for them and building my brand.

All in all, that was a miserable experience, but when I finally resigned, the ink wasn't even dry on my resignation when a recruiter called me and took me to another firm. I was more or less happy there, in the third law firm. But then the firm broke up. I couldn't believe it. What a comedy of errors. Was someone playing a joke on me? Eventually, I decided it didn't make any sense to be trying to fit in to these firms, to be their poster child for special needs, especially if they weren't willing to actually change their way of working. That's when I started Special Needs Law Group.

IT'S A COLD WORLD OUT THERE

Through all the jobs, all the law firms, I saw just how hard it is to sustain employment when you're dealing with the kinds of things I was dealing with on the home front. Yes, there are a lot of employers out there who are sweet and sensitive. But at some point, everybody has had enough. Either your family issues start to impact your job performance—which is understandable—or you just lose out because you can't play the corporate game in the way others can.

The landscape for special needs parents at work was pretty bad back then, in the early 2000s, but it's not that much better today. People are still struggling. There's still no daycare. Parents still have to leave work all the time to do school pickup. No after-school programs for kids like ours. In the Boston area where I live, as in most metropolitan areas, childcare workers and babysitters charge over twenty dollars an hour. I don't know many people who can afford to pay $1,000 a week for childcare, but that's what it would cost for full-time care for kids like mine.

It's a daily struggle, and it impacts everything: our marriages, our health and fitness, even our self-worth. A lot of women, in particular, have a hard time because we came up during the women's movement and were told that we could have it all. It wreaks havoc with our psyche when we realize we can't, even though our friends with typically-developing kids are doing it, raising their kids and having their career as well. It makes us feel inadequate.

But, in certain ways, men have it even worse. They want to do the right thing and be around for their special needs kids, but because they are dads and not moms, their employers *really* don't get it. The business world is so shortsighted when it comes to flexible hours and programs like that. It makes no sense. If they just helped their employees structure their lives in a way that allowed them to do their best work, the payoff would be huge.

The world is changing, but it's not changing fast enough. We need to do what we can to move it along. We can do that collectively by being creative and supportive and always being a community to one another. The more we get people invested in our kids and our families, getting to know us on a personal level, the more people will be willing to help. Hopefully, in time, they'll start to understand that it's not that big of a deal, being the parent of a disabled child—we can still be very productive employees. But the only way we can do this is by sharing our stories, not hiding them, and by continuing to push the envelope.

In my case, as hard as I worked, I never let my work obligations get in the way of choosing to be there for Elizabeth and Caroline. I made a point of spending my weekends with Elizabeth even when there was a lot of work to be done. That's something I've never regretted, even though it slowed down my career and foreclosed certain opportunities for me. It was a choice, *my* choice.

With Caroline, I made sure to always be there to drive her to dance class and to see all of her recitals and events. But, as is common with typically-developing siblings of special needs children, she often got the short end of the stick. I didn't realize at first just how damaging this was to Caroline.

CHAPTER SIX

Caroline

When Caroline was old enough to go to preschool and started to be around other kids, I noticed she was a rather anxious child. She didn't really play with others, preferring to be alone. She was always kind of marching to her own drummer. When I would arrive at school in the afternoon to pick her up, I'd see all the other kids on the rug, listening to story time, and Caroline would be on the other side of the room, playing with the kitchen set on her own.

I moved her around to a lot of different schools, looking for a good fit. She was definitely a unique kid. A very serious child. I didn't really become aware of it until she was about four or five. It was then that she made an offhand comment that took me aback. I don't remember when exactly it happened, but it was definitely a Sunday. We were in Elizabeth's bedroom, and Caroline was with me.

Sundays were family days: I never had a babysitter, nanny, nurse, or aide on a Sunday. It was always just me and the kids.

Elizabeth must have already been about nine or ten at this point. She was getting big, but of course, she was still in diapers. I was changing her, taking care of her, getting her dressed and ready for the day, which took a very long time. Suddenly, Caroline asked me, "Mommy, when am I going to have to start changing Elizabeth's diapers?" I remember the moment like it was yesterday. On the one hand, I was moved by Caroline's big heart. But I was also crushed, internally, to think that Elizabeth and her struggles were already weighing so heavy on Caroline's heart. It wasn't a lighthearted comment. She was looking at me with a furrowed brow, genuinely trying to figure out when it was going to become her responsibility to take care of her big sister.

I just knew that the question had been eating at Caroline. So I told her, right then and there, that she would never have to worry about that. I assured her I had a plan. I was lying through my teeth.

MAKING A VOW TO MYSELF

What I realized on that day was that I needed to start normalizing some things in the household and giving

Caroline the kind of happy childhood experiences she deserved. The typical family things. First things first, I told her that I had a plan, and that she was never going to have to worry about looking after her sister. "Mommy has it all taken care of," I said. All she needed to do was enjoy being Elizabeth's sister.

In reality, I had no such plan. But I resolved then and there to create one. I also realized in that moment just how alone in the world we really are. Wayne wasn't there. Yes, my mother was living with us and was very helpful, but she was getting older. She was showing signs of physical deterioration and was getting more anxious, too. With Elizabeth getting older herself, my mom was having a harder time emotionally dealing with the reality that her granddaughter wasn't just going to "grow out of it."

It's a pretty common dynamic with grandparents of kids with special needs. As loving as they are, it's just a lot easier when their grandkids are young. It's easier to control them and to excuse their behavior. It changes when their grandkids get older.

In the case of my mom, although she was certainly a big help, I knew she wasn't going to be part of the long-term plan with Elizabeth. Even with her and all the help we had around us through Elizabeth's childhood, for the most part, Caroline had grown up seeing me doing it all.

Naturally, it led her to believe that someday it would be her taking over those responsibilities.

The truth is: we *were* alone, and my life *was* burdensome. But I didn't want to let Caroline see that. At the time, she seemed to accept what I said to her. She didn't bring it up again. But inside it continued to eat her alive. It was hard for me to acknowledge, so I probably didn't let myself see how bad it really was. I didn't get it at the time—but she was still filled with anxiety and worry, and would be for many years.

She became what I started thinking of as "the kid with the endless cup." I just could not fill her up. It was never, ever enough. There was never enough of me. Never enough time, energy, money, hours, love, strength. The cup just never got full.

I tried to give Caroline as much of that happy, carefree fun that I could. First, I got her a puppy. She had been begging me for a dog. Then, I organized a family trip to Disney World.

THE HAPPIEST PLACE ON EARTH

I'll never forget that vacation. We went with a big entourage: it was me, the kids, a nurse, a nanny, my mom—and on top of all that, my boyfriend at the time (more to come on him later). It cost me a fortune, of course, to take two helpers, but it was the only option. I went into debt to do it. But traveling without them wouldn't have been possible. Taking care of Elizabeth was still a 24/7 thing. And even Caroline needed a lot of support, with how young she was.

So it was a huge ordeal, and an expensive one—$12,000 if I remember correctly. But it was fabulous. It was just what we needed as a family. Caroline and Elizabeth got to meet their princesses, and we did everything that everybody else did. It didn't matter that Elizabeth was in a wheelchair. We didn't miss a thing. We did it all. Disney World (and Disneyland) really is the happiest place on

Earth. They love their special needs kids there. We were treated like royalty. It was the only place we'd ever been where people were just falling over themselves to be kind to Elizabeth.

She was a queen there, truly. Front of the line for every-thing. She had a special button. Every character stopped to talk to her. She was smiling ear-to-ear the whole time, and Caroline had a blast, too.

Ah, there I go again. This is supposed to be a chapter about Caroline, and I am making her sound like an after-thought. I try and try not to do that. But there's no getting around the facts of the matter. Elizabeth always required so much; Caroline was my do-over kid. Boy, that sucks for her. She knew it, she felt it, she still does—and she gets mad at me for it. Which she should. I will forever feel guilty about not giving Caroline all that she deserved.

Even when we got back from Disney World—and it had gone so well, and I was inspired to keep the good times rolling—I had to ask myself: was I doing it for Caroline, as I had set out to, or was I doing it for Elizabeth? I would take them to the zoo, the park, the beach. We had great times together. Okay, the beach was a disaster. Beaches and wheelchairs don't mix well, and Elizabeth didn't like being hot. But we had a lot of great day trips. We went to Cape Cod, to Maine, even just to Boston for a concert or a ballet.

Elizabeth came to all of Caroline's ballet shows, recitals, everything. In my eyes, we were all in it together. But it wasn't like that for Caroline. She felt very isolated. She didn't have sympathy for me. She never looked at me and said, "Oh, my poor mom, what she goes through, what she has to do." At least she wasn't expressing those emotions and feelings to me.

I used to look around at some of my friends, and their kids, for the most part, just seemed so much nicer, so much closer as a family. Of course, people see things differently on the outside. For all I know, those families were going through the same struggles as we were. But it seemed worse with us. There were times when Caroline would be embarrassed by her sister and not want her to come. Sometimes, she would get upset with me if I brought Elizabeth along when I dropped her off places, or even if I told people that she had a special needs sister.

And yet, one of her really close friends, going all the way back to elementary school, before she started dancing full-time, was a little boy from our neighborhood whose brother was just like Elizabeth. Caroline gravitated to this boy because of what they had in common, the shared experience. What can I say: Caroline is a hard nut to crack. There was definitely a period where she was indifferent toward Elizabeth and somewhat agitated toward her. The older she got, the more she turned away. As the years went on, she utterly rejected Elizabeth—and me, too. Our friends and family noticed and would mention it to me. But deep down I knew Caroline also loved her sister tremendously.

And through it all, I tried—not always successfully, but I tried—to give Caroline the attention that I knew she craved. Honestly, a lot of times, I didn't know what to say to her. I wish someone could have just told me what to do, how to make it all okay.

It did get somewhat better. Some of the best times we spent together, Caroline and I, were the three-and-a-half years when I homeschooled her, from fourth through sixth and part of seventh grade. During that period, it was easier for me to be with Caroline. Elizabeth was going to school, and her health was fairly stable. Caroline, meanwhile, was dancing full-time, twenty hours a week, and when she wasn't dancing, I was homeschooling her. I remember driving her everywhere, while Elizabeth stayed home with the nurse and other helpers, as well as Grammy (my mom).

I was with Caroline *all* the time during those years, going to her shows, watching her do what she loved. What was great about dance was that it was completely her own thing, a world separate from Elizabeth, where she could shine in her own way and didn't have to share the spotlight. The dancing was truly great while it lasted. It was something that made her fully happy. Everything changed, however, when she reached early adolescence.

That's when things started to fall apart for Caroline.

A TURN FOR THE WORSE

Around the age of eleven or twelve, Caroline stopped wanting to dance anymore. This coincided with Elizabeth getting sicker, which made Caroline's anxiety ratchet up.

Then, Caroline started cutting herself. It took me a while to discover what was going on. She wanted to go back to public school, so we did that, because the dance school didn't want her anymore. She had been acting out there and wouldn't listen. She had become a very defiant child, very oppositional.

So we decided to put her into the local middle school, and she was there for a year, but it was sort of half-and-half—half going to school and half homeschooling. That didn't go well at all, so then she went straight into the middle school, which was just a disaster. She started getting into trouble a lot. After I found out that she was cutting, we got two Department of Children and Families complaints, which came right on the heels of Elizabeth getting very sick. It was all just too much. The DCF had gotten involved because of two cutting incidents: one at the dance program and one at school. They knew because Caroline was posting about it on social media.

Meanwhile, I was overwhelmed doing palliative care with Elizabeth. I tried to reason with Caroline: "WTF? What are you doing? Can you just calm down? This makes no sense." In retrospect, I should have listened rather than judged. But this was the culmination of a decade of my just not getting Caroline, not understanding her. She was so different from me. It was too much to handle when I was already so busy going through the worst with Elizabeth.

At this point, Elizabeth was dying, and I knew it. Nobody wanted to talk about it. For better or worse, I tried to talk to Caroline about the fact that her sister was dying. I told her about it. Why did I do that? I was worried that she would later regret her behavior, that she would have a lifetime of guilt about how she treated Elizabeth. I was hoping to turn things around. But it was probably the wrong move. It just made things worse. She didn't believe me, first of all. She thought I was just exaggerating and trying to make her feel guilty and do things she didn't want to do. It was a desperate choice on my part to bring Caroline into all of that. But I was in desperate circumstances.

I was preparing for the worst and pulling away from everybody. What I didn't realize was that Caroline was going through the exact same things, feeling the same way and taking her cues from me. By isolating herself from her friends—by acting out at school and being rude to me and other family and friends, by pushing us away, pushing Elizabeth away—Caroline was starting to cocoon herself, just like I was. We were both pulling inward.

It was a terrible time, that summer of 2012. I had a big fight with my mom and sister at my house. My sister and I got into a total screaming match. She told me she felt sorry for my kids, sorry that they were stuck with me as a mother. We both said terrible things to each other, in front of everyone, including my kids.

We were all feeling the stress. It was a breaking point. My mom moved out, and that meant I had less help than ever, which was just making everything worse. I was exhausted and overwhelmed with everything I needed to do and think about. I was also grief-stricken but didn't recognize it as such. I was just in survival mode.

To see my family turn away from me felt like the ultimate rejection. It felt like they were unhappy with the decisions I was making and didn't think I was doing the right thing by either one of my kids. I realize now that they weren't rejecting me. It's just that they were hurting, too. But no one wanted to talk about was really going on, what was really bothering us. So we found fault with one another in all the wrong places. Like when a couple gets divorced.

On my part, I didn't want my mom and sister and family to have to see what was coming. I didn't feel like I could talk about it with them. I didn't want them to be around for all the pain that lay ahead. And to be honest, I don't think they really wanted to know either: they didn't want to have to admit that Elizabeth was leaving us.

Meanwhile, Wayne was not helping the situation. Yes, he came and visited the kids. But he was unreliable. We never knew if he was going to show up for his scheduled visits or was going to change or cancel them. There were a lot of cancellations with the explanation that his psychiatrist didn't think he was well enough to come right now, didn't think it was "safe" for him to visit. I didn't understand what that meant at the time, but after he was diagnosed with bipolar disorder, it explained a lot of those ups and downs and why he couldn't show up.

It also explained a lot of his behavior. When he *did* come, he often acted pretty strange. There was a lot of wacky talk. It wasn't all a disaster: sometimes, he was fun and normal. And no matter how he acted or what kind of crazy things came out of his mouth, Caroline clung to him. She was crushed every time he disappointed her. She loved her dad and still does. She will defend him vigorously against any perceived slight. But she never felt a safeness and stability with him. Yes, she always wanted to *see* him. She wanted to see him every single day. But from an early age, she was careful not to put herself in situations where she had to rely on him to take care of her.

So it was in this context, this whirlwind of emotion with Wayne and my mom and my sister and myself, that I let Caroline distance herself from me. I let her pull away. I was just too numb and exhausted. I was going into debt. I couldn't work full-time. I just didn't have the energy to deal with any of it, especially to repair my relationship with Caroline.

I did try to find her a therapist, but even that was so difficult. There just aren't a lot of therapists out there who understand sibling stuff. With Caroline, what we were dealing with didn't fit into any of their preexisting boxes. Plus, we had crappy insurance, and even Children's Hospital's psychiatric practice wouldn't accept it. That's how bad this healthcare plan was, and I didn't have $125 an hour to pay every week (let alone twice or three times a week, which is what Caroline needed).

It got to a point where I really, honestly thought I was going to have to hospitalize her. What I didn't realize at the time was that, in the same way that I had been grieving all these little losses throughout my life, she had been grieving as well.

INTERNALIZING OUR EMOTIONS AS THEIR OWN

As special needs parents, we often don't realize the impression we're making on our kids, including our typically-developing kids, even when we're not saying anything out loud. We may not be talking, but they are paying attention; they pick up on our fears and anxieties.

I thought I knew what Caroline needed growing up, but maybe it wasn't enough. I wanted to let her develop as her individual self: not as Elizabeth's sister, but as Caroline Hines. I tried as best I could to give that to her. I arranged all sorts of activities. I taught Sunday school at our church for seven years so that I could be close with her. Then, especially when she was older, I made a point of taking Caroline on mother-daughter trips, just the two of us. We went to Rocking Horse Ranch. I went mother-daughter Girl Scout camping with her, even though, dear Lord, I hated that. I am not a camping person *at all*, but I did it two years in a row with Caroline. I knew how important it was to let her develop her own interests.

I took her to Florida. I took her to Cape Cod, where we went on a whale watch and stayed overnight in the Princess Suite. I really tried to give her that crucial one-on-one time where we could just talk and be ourselves. And it worked: she always seemed to come alive in those moments. I was finally getting to know how funny and smart and beautiful she was. She had a strong sense of self (and fashion!) and was a deep, deep thinker—a real philosopher at heart.

Thinking back to those days now, I wonder what I could have done differently. How could I have been better? And how could I make this up to Caroline? I still think about this. It's not over. How do I apologize now to Caroline? What does it mean for her when I say, "Elizabeth was the love of my life"? I don't mean it as an insult. It's not about favorites. I love Caroline with all my heart. But with Elizabeth, it was just such a different relationship, a different connection.

I look back now on my mother-daughter trips with Caroline and can see how good it was for her to finally be out from under Elizabeth's shadow. But I'm not going to lie: it wasn't easy. It took major effort and sacrifice each and every time to set it up and find someone to be with Elizabeth. Then, when Elizabeth's health problems increased in her teenage years, it became virtually impossible to keep up any semblance of balance. It was *all* Elizabeth, *all* the time.

CHAPTER SEVEN

Elizabeth Grows Up

There had come a point—back when Elizabeth was six, seven, eight—when life had started to settle down. It was a good, long period of stability. We were in the groove. Elizabeth's medical crisis had mostly calmed, and everything was in place with her various providers. Even though she was nonverbal, she was able to have some basic communications through an electronic device. She could use sign language to say "yes" and definitely shook her head no! And I will never forget her laughter as she went hurtling around in her "pony walker," which helped her stand and move around in her space. Most of her time was spent in her purple wheelchair with her name "Elizabeth" embroidered on the seat. She went everywhere in that chair.

I had pretty much figured out how to make this crazy
life work, messy as it all was. Or maybe it was just that
I had gotten used to the craziness. We all had. It was a
fragile equilibrium, but it was something. We had found

a rhythm. I was taking the girls places; we were having these great vacations.

Did I have the money to do all those things? Not really. I was spending so much on Elizabeth's services. Insurance covered some, but there was always more. On the one hand, I was lucky to be living where I was, in Massachusetts. There are a lot of good resources here, and in the Northeast in general. But many of them are private pay. For example, there was a wonderful physical therapist, a wonderful occupational therapist, and even a music therapy program where they come to the home—I looked into all of these, but insurance didn't cover any of it. Then, even for the stuff that insurance *did* cover, they never would allow for home therapy. I always had to schlep Elizabeth everywhere.

And, as I talked about in chapter 3, the way the system worked, if you got your services through insurance, you could never get the best therapists. The real experts had figured out that they could charge five times as much if they didn't accept Medicaid. I don't blame them entirely. I get it. Once they agreed to accept Medicaid, it meant they had to accept every Medicaid patient that came to them. They couldn't say, "Well, I can only see two patients with Medicaid." If they were under contract with CMS (Centers for Medicare and Medicaid Services), they had to agree to work with people regardless of their payor sources. So it made life difficult for them. They would not only get paid a lower rate, but it took a really long time and a lot of paperwork to get paid half or less of what another family paid on the same day of service (if they were private-pay).

So for example, a physical therapy session could be eighty dollars private-pay, and Medicaid would pay thirty-two dollars. But then the therapist might need a whole day to do their billing paperwork to earn that thirty-two dollars. And they could be seeing other patients at that time and earning eighty dollars an hour. On top of that, a lot of times the claims would get rejected for not having the right codes, etc., and the therapist would have to keep submitting them over and over again. Sometimes the claims wouldn't get paid at all. So that's really what private therapists and home-health workers—who have the right intentions and want to try to accept insurance so that they can see all patients—are dealing with. It's not easy.

Many of them are parents of special needs children themselves—that's why they got into this—and they're small business people, struggling to make a living. But the healthcare system is just crushing them. They love what they do, love our kids, and want to commit a certain part of their practice to our kids. But the system makes it very difficult for them to do that. For families like mine, what that meant was that all the best therapists were unavailable to us because they refused Medicaid. Meanwhile, because there was so much wealth in the greater Boston area, there was really no incentive for those therapists to do things differently. They had more than enough privately-paying patients to go around.

I ended up paying out-of-pocket for a lot for Elizabeth. I had friends who could afford to private-pay for much more than I did, who could get excellent around-the-clock care because they had the means to do whatever it took. But I also realized there were people much worse off than me who didn't have any opportunity to supplement what was available through Medicaid. The problem is not that there aren't great resources and equipment out there in the world: wheelchairs that can go on the beach, special bikes for disabled people, and so much more. The problem is that it's all out-of-reach to most. None of those kinds of items are covered by insurance, and they cost a fortune!

In my case, I did what I could. Even though I hated asking, I got some help from my family. I even had to go to Wayne's family at one point when I needed to buy a van for Elizabeth. I couldn't physically get her in and out of the car anymore. But these "wheelchair vans" were really expensive. I couldn't get a loan for the $50,000 I needed for this van, so I "borrowed" $10,000 from Wayne's family to help with a down payment on the vehicle—but I made Wayne pay them back.

I am so grateful to Wayne's parents for the help they gave with the van and other things. The van was Elizabeth's access to the world. Without it, we wouldn't have been able to get out of the house. We'd have been homebound. Wayne's parents recognized how important it was and really helped in our time of need.

It's not a nice feeling to be an adult in your thirties and have to ask for help to take care of your kids. But unfortunately, it's a very common scenario with special needs parents. My situation was like a lot of people's: I relied on Medicaid as much as possible, I asked for help when absolutely necessary, but most of all, I supplemented by paying out-of-pocket.

At the same time, I realized this wasn't sustainable: I couldn't spend everything I had just on Elizabeth. She was only one member of the family, and it wasn't fair to Caroline. I had to have money for Caroline's ballet, for family dinners—even to get my own hair done once in a while! I'm not joking: I didn't get my hair or nails done *for years*. Probably a decade. I did it all at home with a bottle. And I didn't buy new clothes for myself. I wore the same work outfit for like twenty years.

That's just how it was. I was always in survival mode. I couldn't save for college, for Caroline's future, for my own retirement. I couldn't think that far ahead. But I also realized at some point that it couldn't *all* go to Elizabeth. You can't go broke for one person in the family. Especially if it's a long-term situation like it was with her. It wasn't like a cancer scare: we were in this for the long haul. This was our life, so our scarce resources being what they were, and my not being able to work full-time, I needed to be careful.

Every day was a balancing act of trying to set up appropriate one-to-one care so that I could go out with Caroline, or just to have an extra set of hands if I needed to take Elizabeth somewhere. She was getting bigger, so when we were out somewhere, it was a two-person job to change her undergarments because she didn't fit in the baby-changing station in the bathroom anymore. These are the kinds of situations I found myself in as Elizabeth got older. So many new challenges. I had no choice but to pay for helpers, which didn't come cheap. People were looking for twenty to twenty-five dollars per hour for that kind of care. And even at that level, it was hard to get them to choose us over another job that maybe wasn't so messy and hard.

On top of that, even the stuff that *was* covered by Medicaid was a constant battle: I had to fight them to provide the appropriate number of therapeutic hours, the appropriate number of nursing hours, home-health-aide hours... It was crazy: Elizabeth had a degenerative disease, which by definition meant she would deteriorate over time. But the Medicaid folks in charge of evaluating her needs were constantly trying to tell me she was improving and needed fewer services. It was like we were living in Alice's Wonderland where everything was backwards!

But there were always people who would show up from time to time in our lives to help and were just amazing. In my world, I truly believe that God *sent* these people to me. It didn't feel random. It felt like people always came when I needed them. Even though I was desperate and drowning at the time, I recognized how lucky I was to have those several nurses I had for years and years—people who were really there and partnered with me to bring up Elizabeth. She drew them in. She was beautiful and funny and engaging and so easy to love. She really was developing into such a cool person. She loved walking the neighborhood where absolutely everybody knew her and would call out "Hey, Elizabeth!" when we walked by. She enjoyed school and music and laughing at a good joke. We went to the movies often, and she loved the noise and the popcorn—even if she couldn't actually see the movie very well.

So, on the one hand, those were some really great times.

But the truth was, Elizabeth was *not* getting better.

A DEGENERATING SITUATION

Elizabeth was in fact getting worse, as I had always known she would. And she was much bigger now, which made it much harder to take care of her. Just changing her clothes, lifting her up and down, had become really physically challenging for me. We had to get a lift system in the house so that I could continue to take care of her at home. It wasn't cheap, but there was no choice. The nursing agency had rules that the nurses weren't allowed to lift over fifty pounds. So when a patient got older and bigger and went over that weight limit, basically you'd get no more nurse service.

Our nursing agency was really great. This is not a knock

against them. Obviously, it's important that there be regulations in place to protect their people. The agency was quite understanding, actually. They gave me some time to figure out a solution. They were also there to talk options with me. They helped me figure out what kind of equipment I needed and how I was going to handle it.

It was clear that my only option, if I wanted to be able to keep the nursing coverage, was to put in a lift system. It took me about a year-and-a-half to raise the money, not only to put in the lift but also to redo the bathroom so that the lift could transport Elizabeth from her bedroom to the bathroom, and in and out of her wheelchair. Of course, the financial strain was considerable. I had to pay for the bathroom renovations myself. But I was able to get some help from our Department of Public Health—they had a catastrophic illness in children fund—for the work that needed to be done to install the lift system, such as the reinforcement of the ceiling and the extra electrical work. And after a lot of back-and-forth with Medicaid, I was able to get them all the documentation I needed to have them pay for the lift itself. It was a lot of work.

Unfortunately, our bathroom was so small that we couldn't do a Hoyer lift, which is portable; we had to do an overhead lift, which costs more. So that was a big thing. And it couldn't be installed without also reinforcing the ceiling, so I had to get a carpenter to do all of that work.

Through our church I was able to find someone I could afford. Eventually, it all worked out. It took forever to pull it all together, and everybody wanted proof that the other parties were paying for their pieces. Of course, it wasn't fun negotiating all of this, but what choice did I have? If I didn't make it work, I would have lost my nursing care. And, physically, I just wasn't able to take care of Elizabeth 24/7 by myself. At that point, she was truly around-the-clock. Someone had to be with her every night because of the seizures. She required what's called an "awake overnight."

I hate to say it, but without home nursing care, I would have had to put Elizabeth in an institution or a nursing home. And I would have just dropped dead from exhaustion before that happened, honestly. I am so glad I didn't have to do that. But that's the kind of struggle that families like mine have; those are the choices we have to make. I've met parents whose children have behavioral challenges, specifically children with autism spectrum disorder (ASD), and they need all sorts of modifications to their home for safety purposes: alarms, fences, specialty doors.

And just like when I had to redo the bathroom and put in the lift, it's not a one-stop shop. Parents have to become experts, do their detective work, figure out every little piece of the puzzle. There's no one to tell you where to look. It's unique for every child and every family.

Parents and family members really need a system that helps them navigate, especially given how quickly things change. There have been some experiments with programs like No Wrong Door (NWD), a kind of universal gateway to community services and government programs, and Single Entry Point (SEP), which allows families to access service through one agency or organization. In fact, we already have something like this in our state and many states for the elderly: Aging Services Access Points or ASAPs. They're supposed to be there for the disabled as well, but in practice, they're really just focused on the elderly. The challenge is that things that impact the elderly tend to be fairly similar across the board, while things that impact people with disabilities are very disparate. There's such a wide range: you have people with autism, people with Down syndrome, some with physical challenges but no intellectual disability, some who are blind or hard-of-hearing.

It's daunting to try to create a system where there's no wrong door, or only one door, to start getting served. But we should at least be moving in that direction. In essence, it's what I created at my law practice: a door, a navigation system. But, of course, even I cost money. It *should* be free. We should all be able to get services that we're legally entitled to without having to pay somebody to help us figure out how to get those services!

Boy, is it hard. I wish it wasn't. Especially when kids get

older, it's just a lot more difficult to get the support you need. It's sad to say this, but what's cute at age three or four is not cute anymore at age eleven or twelve.

THE TEENAGE YEARS

When Elizabeth went through puberty, life got a lot more challenging, for her and for us. She had a lot of bleeding; her menstruation was very difficult. And, of course, it's not easy to find people who are willing to help with those kinds of things. She was also in a lot of pain, stomach cramping, and just really unhappy. She had a lot of headaches, and her seizures had increased. She could point to her head when she had a headache, and that happened nearly every day as she got older.

I didn't know what to do. Should I put her on birth control? That might help, but it would be risky with her Mito, and her autoimmune system was so messed up. Her blood pressure was always up and down. She had irregular temperatures. We couldn't just do regular hormonal therapy that would have calmed down the periods and the cramping. It didn't help, either, that she had gotten her period early, when she was still only ten. (It's common to experience early menstruation when you take seizure meds.) And from there, it only got harder.

It was during this period that I really struggled with the

school system to get the proper programming Elizabeth needed. A kid like her cost the school district $250,000 a year to educate. Everyone knew it, and it had repercussions. The school board put a lot of pressure on the special education director: *Do we really need to send Elizabeth Hines to Perkins? Do we really need a nurse?*

And because it all happens at the local level—our school districts are made up of local towns and cities, and people's local real-estate taxes are what pay for education—it can start to get very nasty and very political. I was part of an advocacy group in Massachusetts at the time called SPED Watch (as in Special Education Watch), which was started by an amazing woman and advocate named Ellen Chambers. She was a tiger for our kids, a good friend of mine, and I learned a lot from her. We went and met with then-governor Deval Patrick to talk about the special education issues we were having and not being able to get our school districts to pay for the support and resources that our kids needed.

It had become crazy: sometimes the school districts would spend tens of thousands of dollars fighting over a $500 reading program. That's how tense things were and how far we had moved away from a healthy, collaborative process. People around the country were feeling this same way. Some school districts had even started hiring attorneys as their special education directors instead of educators. That's how litigious and dug-in they were.

For me, of course, it was highly personal. The school district was trying to get out of paying for a one-to-one nurse to go to school with Elizabeth every day, but by law, they were required to. And it was more than just the nursing. We were also arguing about the best *place* for her to be educated.

Governor Patrick was generally a strong ally. He did a lot of good for the special needs community. But when I told him my story, his response was: "Oh, but that's just one person, that's just her."

I had to set him straight. "No, it's not," I said. "It's the prevailing attitude in our state, and in our country, because we don't value these children."

Maybe I was being prickly, but by this point, I had gotten quite passionate about my advocacy, and I was tired of having my concerns dismissed. Not long before that meeting with the governor, I had an unpleasant conversation with our special education director where she said something that made me cry. We were talking about Elizabeth's issues and what she needed, and her response was that my daughter was never going to be anything more than a "classroom pet."

Yeah, that really happened. Oh well.

The meeting with Governor Patrick was a much better experience. He was great, but what I'll remember most about that meeting was his actual pet, a little puppy. He had just gotten this cute new dog. It had been all over the local news. Now the puppy was in the meeting with us—and in the middle of all this heavy discussion, with all these high-up people in state government, the little guy was scurrying around, doing his thing, being a dog. He even pooped in the corner of the meeting room.

AN UNEXPECTED TURN OF EVENTS

As many families like mine will understand, just because you have a babysitter—or therapist or nurse—scheduled to come doesn't mean they're guaranteed to be there. You get used to people canceling on you. It sucks: you spend so much time organizing and setting up the coverage you need, and then you get left in the lurch.

There was one day like that when my nurse called in sick, and it was the worst possible day for it because I had to get to a meeting where I was supposed to give a lecture to a group of estate-planning attorneys. The talk was going to be all about special needs families and the basics of special needs planning. So I arrived just in time, exhausted because my help for the morning had fallen through, and

I had been rushing around like a maniac. Then I noticed I had a stain on my shirt from Elizabeth's formula for her G-tube.

I decided it was a good teaching moment. I began my talk with: "Hello everyone, I want to introduce you to the topic of special needs planning and give you some insight into what it's like to be a special needs parent, so that when these families come into your office, into your conference room, you know what's in front of you." Then I pointed out the stain, and the fact that the nurse had called in sick. I also noted that I had my phone right next to me, up at the podium, in case an emergency came up in the middle of the talk. It was my aging mom at home covering for me, and I was worried she wouldn't be able to reach me if there was a problem.

It may have seemed weird to have a phone at the podium. But to me that was nothing new. There had been so many times in my career when I had *no* coverage and my kids had to come with me to meetings, conferences, banquets. Times when I just didn't have the choice. I didn't have any backup, and I needed to go to these things. To this day, people will say, "Hey Annie, remember that time at the banquet when Elizabeth and Caroline were there and they were all dressed up." I appreciate those memories, and for the most part, my colleagues—and even many judges—were amazing in these situations. So warm and understanding and inviting. But it was still a different world than what most people could even imagine.

"Hopefully," I told the crowd, "that gives you a bit of an idea of what my life is like. You have to understand that, as a group, special needs parents are very, very tired. So unlike your other estate-planning clients, when you ask us to do things, think to yourself first...Are these things that you could do *for* them? Before you send them home with twelve pieces of homework, documents to provide, etc., first ask yourself, 'What can I do to help them get this planning done, and make life, and this project, a little easier for them?'"

Many of them had never thought of it that way before. They gave me a standing ovation, and then I had a whole bunch of people come up afterwards to ask me questions. I needed to go, I had things to do—pick up Caroline, relieve my mom—but when I finally pulled myself away and exited the room where I had been speaking, I found myself cornered by Mark Worthington. He wanted to get me all alone and talk to me.

I knew who Mark was. He was pretty well-known in our state, a very knowledgeable tax and trust attorney, and the former president of our Mass chapter of NAELA (National Academy of Elder Law Attorneys). He didn't know anything about me, but he proceeded to keep me there for the next thirty minutes, sharing all these personal things with me. He told me his whole life story, that he had just gotten a divorce, that his partnership had blown up, that his daughter had been sick with Lyme disease. Finally, he asked me to speak at another event. I said yes, mostly because I just needed to get away. The next day I emailed him and backpedaled: "You know, that's really far for me, and it's early in the morning. I can't do that, I'm not going to be able to do that." But he begged, and pleaded, and whined, so I did.

Then, after that event, he found all these reasons for us to have coffee. He wanted to talk to me about qualified disability trusts and special tax provisions. No joke. He was so enamored because I would actually have these conversations with him. Before long, coffee turned into lunch, and lunch turned into a movie. After about seven or eight months of this, I said to him, "You do realize we're dating, right?" He paused for a moment and then said, "Oh yeah, okay."

A few months later, he asked me to marry him. The ring was big. Mark was very handsome and romantic kneeling down by the Christmas tree. He had gotten all dressed up in a suit, even though I was still in my pajamas. The kids were in bed; it was so quiet in the house. It was a beautiful moment. I said yes. I did have thoughts about whether this was really the right thing at the right time.

I also had thoughts about his sanity! But there was the guy, and there was the big ring—and he was so cute and so sweet, and obviously loved me so much. I just had to say yes.

Chapter Eight

Decisions

Elizabeth turned sixteen at the end of May 2012. By this point, she had been having a lot more seizures, getting sick a lot more often, and needing more nursing care. She was having difficulty keeping her oxygen up and just didn't have a lot of energy. She was still enjoying her time at school, but her hospital stays were increasing.

For her birthday party, we had a Sweet Sixteen celebration at a local restaurant, with a DJ and everything. A bunch of friends came. We danced, ate, and had a ball. Mark was there, and this was back before we were a "thing." It was actually his first time meeting Elizabeth. He had said he would like to meet her, so I invited him to the party. I still remember how he showed up with a big coffee stain down the front of his shirt. When I say a big stain, I'm talking *enormous*.

That's Mark. He's *often* got coffee stains down his shirt. He's like an absent-minded professor, so deep in his head that he doesn't pay attention to stuff like that. He's a brilliant legal mind, but he forgets the basics and trips over things a lot. You gotta love him. Initially, I tried to set him up with a friend of mine who was at the party. I sat him next to her, but they were having none of each other. Elizabeth, on the other hand, immediately loved him. She loved physical comedy when people were always hurting themselves, and she was a great judge of character! Mark stayed until the very end of the party. It was a wonderful time, and I still have all the great photos and videos from that day.

Elizabeth had a blast. But then, as the summer wore on, she started to have more difficulties. I dreaded the fall, because that's when Elizabeth would get the flu or some other respiratory infection. But with her, it wasn't just flu. It could turn into pneumonia and all the respiratory challenges that went with that. Even a simple cold could take her down for weeks. The weather didn't help either. It was hard enough to do anything with Elizabeth, but to have to dress her up for the cold in her wheelchair and get her in and out of the house with the ice and snow was overwhelming.

I hadn't always dreaded the fall like this. Back when I was growing up, I used to love the season: the apples, the leaves, the crisp smell in the air. Everything just seemed fresh. I liked it much more than spring. But with Elizabeth, that all went away. Fall meant winter was coming, and winter meant illness. Every time she got sick, it just knocked her down a little further and made it that much harder for her to come back. Through 2012 and into the new year, she was in the hospital a lot. And by February or March of 2013, it had just been pneumonia after pneumonia, and lots and lots of seizures. The seizures had become intractable by this point, and she was maxed out on multiple medications. When Elizabeth was sick, her whole body fell apart. That's the way it is with Mito kids. She wouldn't even stop on the regular floor at the hospital. It was straight to the ICU every time.

But I had already made the decision to stop seeing all the specialists and traveling into Boston all the time. The doctors at the hospital had long since been able to add anything to Elizabeth's life or even her comfort. There had been so many of them over the years. At one point, we had been seeing twelve different specialists—cardiologist, gastroenterologist, neurologist, the list just went on and on—and they all wanted to see her every six months. It had gotten to be too much. Elizabeth was miserable. She hated the hospital. She would start crying and fussing when we pulled up to the front door. She knew where she was. Even though she couldn't see that well, the smell and the sound totally got to her.

I couldn't take it anymore. I couldn't make her miserable for no reason. She was seeing very little benefit from all these specialists. They weren't really adding medications or new treatment plans. They were just barely trying to keep her stable—and they were losing that battle.

Elizabeth's pediatrician, Dr. Mike McKenzie, who was my key quarterback, was completely on board with my decision about cutting back on those visits to the specialists. He had become my care coordinator, my home base. He helped us manage her symptoms from home. He even made home visits, him and his wife, Lee. She was a child psychologist. They were both so great to us. They'd come to the house together at the end of the day to see her so that I wouldn't have to try to haul Elizabeth, who was sick as a dog, into the doctor's office.

I'll forever be grateful to them for that. It is virtually unheard of to get home visits. I knew they weren't getting insurance to reimburse them; they were just being good souls. I had become so close with them, and they had become so intimate with Elizabeth's care, that we were now on a first-name basis. It wasn't the usual relationship that families have with their pediatrician. I was lucky to have them.

But we still had to go to the hospital a fair amount, especially when Elizabeth was really sick. One day we were there and the doctors were doing their rounds. They asked me to join them for a quick conference outside Elizabeth's room. They told me how bad things had gotten. She was at the point, they said, where there was really nothing left to do. Her swallow had become so weak that she was aspirating her own saliva—in other words, she couldn't swallow her own spit safely anymore.

Her body was attacking her and making her sick. What could be done about it? "Well," they said, "we can take out her saliva glands." I thought about it for a moment. I knew what would happen: we'd try to solve one thing, and it would create a whole new problem. Even when people just have partially-blocked saliva glands, they have a lot of issues with dry mouth. I couldn't imagine how bad it would be to have *no* saliva glands at all.

That was the story of Elizabeth's life: she'd start a new treatment, and the treatment itself would sometimes work but led to all these new adverse effects. There was always a hidden cost, and by this point, every medical decision that we made had to take into consideration not just the good that would come from it but also the bad. I decided against surgery to remove the salivary glands. By early spring, I knew that we were rounding the curve and the end was near. We had been working with the palliative care team at Children's, who were amazing and very supportive.

In August 2013, I signed a "comfort care" form, which basically instructs the doctors to take no more extreme measures. It's similar to a DNR, or Do Not Resuscitate, document. But it's more than that: it's about what the family wants. We decided that, above all, we wanted Elizabeth to not have to suffer any pain; we would keep treating infections until we got to the point where it was no longer helping. These are, of course, agonizing decisions—but again, we had the support and understanding of the extraordinary hospital team through it all. The hardest part, though, is speaking for someone who cannot speak for themselves. Trying to interpret what her wishes or choices would be was gut wrenching for me.

Elizabeth got amazing, magnificent care. The doctors and nurses there were awe-inspiring. They loved and took care of *me*, as well. For example, they helped me find resources for Caroline. Because my mom wasn't living with me at the time, Caroline had to come everywhere with me and stayed overnight at the hospital with me a few times. The staff there saw how angry and difficult she was getting. She was so rude to everybody, especially me. She was a storm of anxiety and emotion—a tempest in a teapot.

But they got it. They understood and did everything they could to help Caroline, including helping me find resources for counseling, support groups, and more. They were amazing and were always checking in with how I was doing, how Caroline was doing.

Through thick and thin, these nurses serve not just their patients but the whole family. They do it with such honor and dignity. Can you imagine what it must be like for them? It's like living in a constant war zone. I say this in the figurative sense, but there was one day when this expression took on a new meaning.

A DAY FROM HELL

We were in the hospital, in what they call "step-down intensive care"—which is the intermediate care unit—when the Boston Marathon bombing happened and the city went on lockdown as the police searched for the suspects. They actually stopped letting people into the hospital because it was such madness. One of the bombing victims was there, the little girl who lost her brother and lost her leg. We didn't know any of this at the time—nobody was telling us anything—but Mark couldn't get to us. The authorities had shut down all the streets leading up to the hospital. They weren't letting any cars in, not only because they were searching the area, but also to protect the victims in the hospital.

Mark ended up parking outside the city limits, where some very kind gentleman who owned a Dunkin' Donuts let him park his car. Eventually Mark found a cab that brought him close to the hospital, and then he walked the rest of the way. It took him hours to get to us. Thankfully, Caroline was safe and being taken care of by my mom and sister at my sister's house. They had come to pick her up late the night before the city was shut down. Even though they were still mad at me, and we were still kind of in this family fight, they were there for me and Caroline. They showed up.

When I think back to that day, I somehow conflate the tragedy going on outside the hospital walls, in the streets, and the personal trauma we were experiencing with Elizabeth's deteriorating health. I guess that's a common phenomenon: people identify current events with whatever's going on in their own life at the time.

That was in April. A month later, we celebrated Elizabeth's seventeenth birthday, and then she went to her school prom. Mark and Elizabeth's teacher and her nurses convinced me to let her go to the prom, with her oxygen and everything. I was so nervous because of how fragile she was at the time. I just didn't want to let her out of my sight, but she went and had a great time. I'm glad everybody persuaded me. I wasn't going to let her do it, but it ended up being a wonderful experience for her.

Her prom date was a boy named Auddie, whose mom I

still talk to from time to time. Elizabeth's teacher, Jodi, drove the van. The nurses were not allowed to drive Elizabeth around, so I needed two people. Jodi came all the way out from school, picked up Elizabeth, and drove our van with her and her nurse, Trish. Trish had changed around her whole schedule so that she could escort Elizabeth to the prom. She and Jodi helped out in that way because they knew how important it was for Elizabeth to have a regular, grownup prom night, just like every kid, without her mom there.

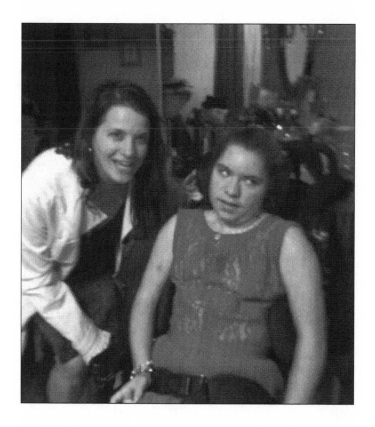

Both Elizabeth and Trish got dressed up in fancy prom attire. Elizabeth wore a beautiful red dress. It was gorgeous on her. Trish had also brought a friend along with her to our house to help do Elizabeth's hair for the night. She wore it in a beautiful up-do—again, like any other teenage girl going to prom. Before they arrived officially in the prom area (previously the Perkins gym!), Auddie gave her a corsage, and she was just beaming from ear to ear. When I look back at my pictures and video of that day—of Elizabeth getting her hair done, and Auddie escorting her to the prom—I am just so grateful for my village that showed up for her.

And to think that I almost didn't let her attend. But it wasn't just that I was being dramatic or paranoid. I knew she wasn't going to live much longer. When we celebrated her birthday, I really believed it would be her last one. But no one wanted to hear that. Everyone kept saying, "No, no, she's fine, she's going to be fine." I guess they were trying to be positive, but it made me feel alone, like I had nobody to talk about my fears and concerns with—nobody wanted to discuss it.

To me, it was clear where this was all headed. There was just no place to go, no path that didn't end badly. That summer we were in and out of hospital nonstop. But then, September was the really bad month. It was when I signed the DNR comfort care measures. Then, the school found out about the comfort-care forms—I guess a nurse must have alerted them—and they contacted me about it. They said they needed to know if Elizabeth was dying. They told me it might not be safe for her to come to school anymore.

I was mad at the nurses for leaking this information to the school, but what I didn't realize then was that the nurses—some of whom, like Trish and Caterina, had been with us for years and years—were hurting, too. They were losing somebody *they* loved, and they needed to talk about it. They probably felt like they couldn't talk about it with me, rightfully so. It wouldn't have been appropriate for them to look to me for support. They just didn't have a good place to go with all of their feelings, which is why I guess they ended up talking about everything with the folks at school. I get it. The nurses were not made of stone. They had feelings, too, and they needed some place to turn. These were people who had watched Elizabeth for years and helped her grow up.

Still, hearing that I might have to take Elizabeth out of school freaked me out. I understand the school had to worry about its own liabilities, but Perkins was really the only joy in Elizabeth's life, besides her family and her dog. She loved the school. She had so many friends there, and she adored her teacher, Jodi. Then there was her amazing music teacher, John, who got her to actually use her voice to make sounds that sounded like singing. The school was a magical place. I just couldn't risk losing it.

So I lied. I told them I never signed any comfort-care form. "Elizabeth's fine," I said. "She's not dying. Don't worry, everything's fine." I'm not proud of having lied to them. I violated their trust, but I had to do what I believed was best for Elizabeth.

"You've known me for years," I said. "It's been like eight years that Elizabeth's been coming to school here. You know I'm not going to send her in sick. I'm not going to send her to school if she's not safe. So you don't have to worry about that. Those decisions will be made." That convinced them. It was true that I had built up a lot of trust. But I violated their trust by not telling them the truth in that moment.

They had lost a student the year before, and it had been very traumatic for the whole school. So they didn't want to go through that again. I understand: it's very scary for everyone involved. I get that they don't want to have to see all that. But when you're the parent of the kid who's going to die, you have different priorities.

CHAPTER NINE

A Good Death

In September, we went into hospice services. We were at the point where, other than going to school, Elizabeth wasn't really doing anything. She just kind of hung out in her wheelchair. Again, with Mito, she was exhausted. It took up all her energy just to enjoy her day at school. She needed oxygen quite a bit and had to carry a tank around with her. She required oxygen overnight when she was sleeping. And on the weekends, she spent a lot of time in bed.

We had stepped up the nursing care; she was almost 24/7 at that point. We did as much as we could. It hadn't helped that one of our nurses had gotten injured over the summer and couldn't work. Elizabeth needed "awake overnight" care, but three to four nights a week I had no one. So, I was staying up twenty-four hours and then having to go to work. Mark was trying to help, too—he was living in the house now, ever since we had gotten engaged under the Christmas tree in December 2012—but he could only do so much.

Now, we were a month away from our wedding. We had pushed the wedding up because of Elizabeth's decline. I really, really wanted her to be there. Deep down, I also knew—but had such a huge fear in the back of my mind that I almost wouldn't admit this to myself—that if Elizabeth died, I wouldn't be able to go through with marrying Mark. I probably would have walked away from the situation altogether.

Which is why it meant so much to actually get married, to make that kind of commitment to him in church during this time of our life. It definitely solidified our bond. I mean, think about it from Mark's perspective. He walked into a real shit show. Who does that? Either he was amazing or the stupidest person on the planet. At the time, I couldn't tell which one it was. Now, of course, I know the answer: he's amazing.

We had a relatively small wedding. About eighty close friends and family members. It was October 26, 2013. Elizabeth had two nurses who took shifts taking care of her. She was there with her oxygen, her G-tube pump, her suction machine: all the things she needed to get through a few hours. After the ceremony, we had a reception right there in the church hall, to make life easier. We knew a long, drawn-out event would be impossible with Elizabeth.

But boy am I glad that she could be there. All three of our daughters—Mark's daughter from his previous marriage and my girls—were wearing off-white dresses that matched my wedding gown. They looked so beautiful. I remember us all getting dressed together in the church. I had all these helpers for Elizabeth, and even some of the other nurses, who weren't officially on duty, came to visit that night and be with us for the wedding. They all loved Elizabeth. And they loved Mark, thought he was the greatest.

What a night. What a celebration. I got to dance with Elizabeth in her wheelchair. We danced to Sister Sledge's "We Are Family." Such a great song for a family wedding. Then the song that I picked for our official wedding song was Frank Sinatra's "All The Way." It goes: "When some somebody loves you, they need to love you all the way." That meant so much to me because it described Mark perfectly. He really had gone all-in. For him, there was just no boundary there. He loved me and the kids so thoroughly and completely.

I think he just saw something in me and fell in love with me and my kids, even though it was a sad situation. In some ways, he was a supporting actor in the play that was my life at that time. But he was a *strong*, strong supporting actor. He was the one who I got all my lines from, the base that I could work off of. He did all the things I just couldn't get done during that time: he kept the practice going, ordered laundry service, got food delivered. He just did whatever was needed for us to survive, and he really bonded with my daughters.

He got very close with Caroline, and Elizabeth just loved him. She was always such a good judge of character. She would tell me right away, for example, if she didn't like a new nurse who was assigned to our case. If she sensed that the person didn't get her or respect her, she would just completely reject them. She'd cry when they came over, wouldn't look at them, and would turn away when they tried to talk to her. Even though she couldn't speak, she'd give all kinds of clues with her body language that this was not a preferred person in her life.

But Mark, she just loved. She laughed at every stupid joke and dumb thing he did. And it was really beautiful to see, because her approval helped *me* see what a great guy Mark was.

He was my Best Supporting Actor, and I needed him more than ever in those weeks after we put Elizabeth into hospice care. I was at my wit's end. All the pressure was starting to take a toll on my health. The hospice care for Elizabeth was just okay. Maybe that system works better for kids who can verbalize what they want, who can express their pain. But in our case, the hospice nurses mostly just made a bad situation worse. One of them came in and all she had to say was, "Oh my God, this is so sad." Really? And she's supposed to be the professional!

It's ironic: the only person I felt like I could really talk to about what we were going through during this time was not part of the hospice team at all, but rather our old, local pediatrician, Dr. Mike. He had been taking care of Elizabeth since she was two, and Caroline since she was born, so he knew us very well. He also had some experience working with kids with special healthcare needs, but really, it was more that he's just a good human being. I had been talking to him through the years about all these questions I had, like "how much is too much?" and "how do you know when to stop?" He was one of the few people willing to have those kinds of discussions with me without making me feel bad for depressing him.

How ridiculous is it that the mother of the dying child has to feel bad for talking about it? It's not like I was being grim just for kicks. I needed to be realistic: it was just a matter of time. How long was this going to go on? There was no place for me to talk about what I was going through, about the dying process. No support group for this, for people whose kids are dying. There's only a support group for kids who are already gone.

Between September and November 2013, Elizabeth had several pneumonias, and then the worst began. On November 13th, I got a call from the school. She had been sick and was taking antibiotics for the pneumonia. Then she had gotten better, and so we sent her back to school, but she was still feeling kind of blah. I got the call from school, and they told me she was really not doing well. They said I needed to come right away. This happened just as I was leaving bankruptcy court, which nobody else knew about.

Elizabeth never went back to school after that. The doctor came over. My mom and sister came over. Elizabeth had a raging fever. It was pneumonia again. She hadn't even recovered from the last one. It had only been about three weeks. The combination of her failing immune system and not being able to swallow made these episodes inevitable. Her muscles in her throat were so weak that the saliva was just getting into her lungs and infecting her over and over again. There was nothing we could do to stop it.

We had stopped feeding her food a few months before. That was devastating to me and my whole family, and to Elizabeth herself, because food was one of the few things that she got great enjoyment out of. She never ate for nutrition, but she did eat for pleasure. Especially in an Italian family like mine, food is such a part of the culture. It's an integral piece of life, of our celebrations, and of our sad times as well. The dinner table is the center of it all. So to not have that anymore had been a huge loss.

But now the real loss, the one that I knew was coming someday, was around the corner. Mark had to call Wayne and tell him that he needed to get his ass up to Natick, that Elizabeth was dying. I had tried first, and initially, Wayne said no, he was too busy with work. But eventually he did come. He asked one of his friends to join him, and I think that helped. His friend, Steve, was very supportive to him, and it made a big difference.

From that point on, everyone came and paid their respects. I kept Caroline home from school. My family came and pretty much stayed from there on out. A lot of people came to say goodbye: folks who had known and loved Elizabeth from school, as well as friends in the town and neighborhood. Her teacher, Jodi, came and read to her. In fact, Perkins gave Jodi time off so that she could be there every day with Elizabeth, which was amazing. Lots of people brought food. That's what they do.

Me? I just sat in a recliner chair next to Elizabeth's bed for five days straight. I barely left that chair at all. All I wanted was to be close and hold her. Her skin was so hot to the touch. She had an infection and was just burning up the whole time. It was hard to keep her comfortable, but we were giving her morphine for the pain. The nurses and hospice team had given us a pain management kit.

The pneumonia started on a Wednesday. Friday night, she woke up for a little while and was alert. We had stopped giving her meds, and everything was shutting down, so when she woke up, I started to panic. Had we made a huge mistake? Suddenly, I had an impulse to reverse course and get her G-tube going again, feed her, give her medicine. I thought that I had done the wrong thing. Maybe there was still hope that she could get better? There wasn't. But by that point I was just a crazy person. I even heard a nurse say to my mom that I was losing it. I really was. They started giving me some Ativan or something to try to keep me calm.

Ultimately, the doctors helped me come to the realization of what a mistake it would be to drag this out any longer. The end was inevitable, and it would only make it harder on Elizabeth over the long haul. I have to give credit to the doctors for the way they helped me navigate this decision-making process. They never tried to talk me out of anything. They let me make my own decisions, but they did also guide me. During those last few days, they were on the phone with me all the time. I had constant support.

It was a Wednesday night that I decided to stop care. After talking to Dr. Mike, I was convinced it was time. Elizabeth was ready. But was I ready? It felt like the whole world was closing in on me. I just didn't know what to do. I needed a few minutes to myself, so I went out on my back porch. I didn't have a jacket on, and this was November in New England. It was really cold; my teeth were chattering. I sat there for probably ten or fifteen minutes, with my brain furiously going through lists, data points, trying to figure out what I should do. It was a lonely moment really, because nobody else could make the decision for me. I was the only one who could speak for Elizabeth. And she didn't have any way of telling us that she was ready to go.

It was at that moment that my mom came out on the porch and sat down with me. She didn't say a word, but all of a sudden, I didn't feel lonely anymore. She didn't need to say anything or help me weigh the pros and cons. Her presence was enough. We cried a little bit, and she put her hand on my shoulder. A minute later, I went back inside the house and told everyone that I had made my decision.

Elizabeth's alertness hadn't lasted long. Soon after that window of time where she had woken up and seemed lucid, she went back to sleep again and that was that.

She died on Monday morning.

It was just like on TV, with the stupid sound of the monitor, the beep of the heart monitor turning into a flat-line noise.

The nurse who was with her, who I love dearly, said something in the moment like, "And we're done." We all felt that way. We were all just so tired, so sad. Then, I sat with Elizabeth and waited for Dr. Mike to come and pronounce her dead. He left his practice in the middle of a busy Monday morning to come out and sign the death certificate so that we wouldn't have to bring her to the hospital. We had arranged it all in advance, and he had talked me through all the details.

It represented a turning point, from my feeling in the beginning like I was never getting any information from the doctors to feeling at the end like I had this great collaborative team: the nurses and the nursing agency, the team at Children's, the hospice people, and Dr. Mike and his wife Leigh. They gave me everything I needed to help me plan and prepare. Mike had his share of special needs kids in his practice, more so than the average doctor. So it was fitting that he would come and be there for me.

After Elizabeth passed, I had to wait for the funeral home to come and get her body. They let me walk down with her to their vehicle. They didn't cover her up or anything, just put a blanket on her. She looked like she was sleeping. As upsetting as it all was, I knew it was the right thing—for

Elizabeth to be at home, surrounded by her family, and for us all to be in a calm, peaceful environment like that, to say our goodbyes together.

One amazing detail that I will never forget: just twelve hours before Elizabeth passed, our dog had started howling in the middle of the night. It was like she knew. I was in Elizabeth's room at the time, and Caroline had come in to tell me the dog was freaking out and not calming down. It was really Caroline's dog, and she was worried about her: the dog was sad and out of sorts. We all were. But it had been an especially brutal time for Caroline. Five long days at home with people coming and going, just waiting for Elizabeth to pass. I could see that Caroline was wracked with grief; it was almost too painful to see her that way.

Even though there were a lot of people around in the house, it was a very lonely experience—not something you can fully share. Nobody knows your heart. But I will never forget that image of Caroline lying down on the bed next to her sister right before Elizabeth died, to say her last goodbyes. She was hugging her and sobbing.

It was a Sunday that Caroline got on that bed with Elizabeth. It feels fitting that it was a Sunday, which had always been our family day. And now it was on this cold Sunday in November that I held Elizabeth in my lap for the last time. It was also the day that the dog got upset. It may sound strange, but it was like the whole family came together one last time to celebrate our Sunday family day.

All in all, the period leading up to Elizabeth's passing was the longest five days of my life. I was just so numb at that point. My brain couldn't take anymore. When I think back to that November morning, it's almost like I'm watching a movie. Like it was all happening to someone else. Had it all just been a dream? No, it was real. But in a way, it was also my personal nightmare. I was destined to relive it over and over in my mind.

CHAPTER TEN

After

Elizabeth was the love of my life.

I know most people say their husband or their wife is the love of their life. But for me, I know it was her. Elizabeth just totally got me, and I got her. We spent a lot of time alone together, she and I. She was a good daughter. Even though she was so disabled, she was incredibly powerful in her way, and so good to me—and good *for* me.

She taught me so much, and not in that stupid, goofy way that people like to say. She really did help me learn about life. For one thing, she brought me to this great profession that I love. I get to meet so many awesome people because of her. I still talk to her teacher, Jodi. We stayed friends. Elizabeth had such an impact on Jodi and on so many people. It's amazing how somebody who was nonverbal could be so impactful. I don't think that's true of every special needs kid. Elizabeth was a light. She really was.

The following Easter, our pastor spoke about her, about the fact that she was called to God. He talked about how perfect she was, how perfect it is to be with God. I truly believe that, and it gives me great comfort. I think about her in Heaven, talking, running, doing all the things she couldn't do when she was here with us.

I still love her so much. Nothing is ever diminished. Never.

THE QUIET AFTER THE STORM

After Elizabeth passed, after the parade of people in our house, suddenly everybody was gone. The house was empty. A crew came and took away all her medical equipment. They removed her hospital bed, her medicines, everything. It was weird. Then I had to go to the funeral home and pick out a casket. I couldn't even think. I don't really remember much about it. It felt so surreal: *What am I doing here, picking out a coffin? What am I even supposed to be asking for?*

There were all these decisions to be made, about what pictures to show, what songs to play, what flowers to buy. Somehow it all got done, but for the life of me, I don't know how. I don't remember making any decisions about the funeral. I barely remember the wake. But I know that many people came. It was such a tribute to Elizabeth and our family that so many people attended.

I do remember one moment that really touched me. A large group of students from the Perkins School for the Blind came out with their teachers and their aides and helpers. The sheer coordination required to pull that off was amazing. Each and every one of them came up to me and told me something wonderful they remembered about Elizabeth. Her music teacher John, in particular, had been so touched by her as a student. I honestly never realized Elizabeth had friends. When you have a kid with disabilities who's so blocked in terms of communication, and so blocked physically from the world, it's hard to even think about it like that. But here these people were, these other disabled, blind children coming up to me in their own way and telling me beautiful things about my daughter.

I just cried for three straight hours. I had considered splitting up the wake into two sessions, which people sometimes do when it's a big crowd. But I knew I couldn't handle that. So we just made it one long three-hour session. I cried and cried. At one point, I had snot running down my nose that I didn't even notice, and Mark was right there next to me with a tissue, wiping my nose for me as I was trying to talk to people and hug them. Yeah, it was quite a scene.

All in all, it felt like the longest week of my life. We buried her on Friday, four days after she passed. It was raining outside, and I remember waking up that morning and thinking that I just wanted it to rain forever. I never wanted the sun to shine again. It felt right somehow, appropriate, that it was so cold out. It was the kind of November cold that just sits in your bones and makes you hurt, you know?

But then I started thinking about how Elizabeth was going to be cold in the ground, and it made me upset and sick to my stomach. I literally thought I was going to throw up. I couldn't believe there was such a thing in this world as a children's coffin. How terrible that it even exists. But there it was, and she was inside of it, under the cold, cold dirt.

I still think about that. It's so creepy. I think about her being down there, under the ground, and I just can't handle it. When we buried her, I thought I was ready. I was so full of myself thinking about how smart I was that I had made all these preparations and how I was going to be ready when the time came. I wasn't ready. I'm still not ready.

THE ZOMBIE YEAR

In the months after Elizabeth died, in fact for a whole year after, I was like a dead person, just walking around like a zombie. I still did my job; I connected with people. But it was all a charade. I struggled every morning just to get out of bed and go to work. I remember spending a lot of time that winter lying on my bed, doing nothing, just staring at the ceiling. Mark took up the slack in terms of keeping the household running, getting Caroline back and forth from school, calling in laundry service, having meals delivered. He was amazing. Me, I just couldn't get up. It was like my arms and legs and head were all so heavy, weighing me down. It took so much energy just to lift myself up out of bed, get my clothes on, and get out the door.

People had stopped visiting. For them, it was all over. For me, it was still such a difficult time. I couldn't think. Grief is funny that way, how it hits you. It's not always about the crying. It's not like you're in the same excruciating pain and agony that you were. But the grief is still there, it's deep, and it impacts you in other ways: it interferes with your memory, your ability to think and process information.

Grief comes like the ocean: it crashes over you like waves, then retreats for a little while, then comes back again. In the same way that the waves reshape the shoreline, my grief would slowly reshape my life. It's a very gradual transition, just like with the seascape, but very powerful. It is the process of becoming something else.

At some point, almost a year after Elizabeth's death, I was able to get my footing again. The sand had come back, and the tide had gone out. The waves weren't as strong. Whereas earlier, I felt like I was drowning, now the ocean was calm, and I could catch my breath. I started to think clearly again, and to try to rediscover who I was in life and why I was doing what I was doing.

QUESTIONING EVERYTHING

If I wasn't Elizabeth's mom anymore, who was I? The relationship had defined me for so long, almost my entire adult life. I had her right after I graduated from law school. It had been school, school, school, school, school, married, baby. My whole identity as an adult was being Elizabeth's mother. Without it, I was lost. I started to perform a kind of inventory of self. Yes, I was an attorney, but did I still want to do that kind of work? Did I want to get another job instead? Did I want to shut my practice down?

I was also a wife. Did I want to stay married to Mark? I loved him, but part of me wanted to just sell everything, shed all the trapping of my previous life, and move away with Caroline. I know how harsh that sounds, and I'm certainly glad I didn't do that, didn't act on those impulses. But at the time, I just didn't have anything left. As devoted as Mark had been to me, I didn't think I had it in me to love him the way he loved me. I was struggling just to love

Caroline. It's awful, but it's the truth. I was struggling to feel *anything* at that time.

Caroline knew it, too. She was in a lot of pain herself, understandably. In fact, she was in a lot more pain that I had ever, ever imagined. The spring after Elizabeth died, Caroline revealed to me that she had been molested, for many years, by my old boyfriend—the one who had come to Disney World with us, the one I was with before I met Mark.

I immediately went to the police and the district attorney. But they wouldn't go forward the case because Caroline was so fragile. Everyone was worried about what she might do to herself, including her therapist. There was a lot going on: Caroline had stopped taking showers and was having a really hard time at school. I had gotten her into a very small Catholic high school because I didn't want her at the big high school in Natick with 3,500 other kids. I just knew she would get lost there, like she had in middle school.

But even at the smaller Catholic school, she had a tough time. For two solid years, she struggled. When she opened up to me about the abuse she had endured, I didn't put any pressure on her to go forward to the police—but I was happy that we had reported it, and that they were on it. Fortunately, the laws in our state are such that she can come forward for many, many years. She has time to think about this and decide if she wants to do something about it.

But at the time that she told me what happened, all I could think of was how angry I was at the person who did this to my daughter, and how guilty I felt for having let it happen. It killed me, but how could I have known? This guy hadn't even been with us very much. He didn't live with us. He was rarely alone with Caroline. It must have always happened right under my nose, when I was busy taking care of Elizabeth.

It made me furious that he had taken advantage that way. All along, I had believed that Caroline was cutting herself out of grief and anxiety over what was going on with her sister. I'm sure that was part of it. But now I realized there was much more going on.

A PERFECT STORM

It didn't help that we were in such dire straits financially during this period. We were in the thick of the bankruptcy process and often had to go to court. We tried to sell the house but couldn't get what we wanted for it. Eventually, we got set up with a repayment plan for the mortgage. It was difficult—this was a lean time for Mark and me—but once the installment plan was in place, it made me feel better about the whole situation.

My family—my mom, my sister—were there for me during this time, but they also kept a distance. Everyone did. I get it now: it's just too painful. As much as people say they want to help, the reality of losing a child is just so devastating and traumatic that it's too much to engage with. It's a psychological hurdle, and most people can't make that leap. Unless they've been there themselves. I had known several people in my life who'd lost their children before me. I had been to their funerals. The beautiful thing is that every single one of those moms came to Elizabeth's wake and funeral. They all showed up for me, because they knew. They'd been through it, too. But they were the exception. The natural instinct is to turn away, and that's what a lot of people did.

LIFE MARCHES ON

I was surprised at the number of friends, or people I had considered friends, who didn't reach out after Elizabeth passed. They were there for me during her active dying phase. And then right after, people came for a while to pay their respects. But then it was all over so quickly. Everybody just went on with their lives. I couldn't understand it. Was I also supposed to move on so quickly? How do people do that? I couldn't wrap my head around living without Elizabeth in my world.

When we had a luncheon at a local restaurant on the Friday morning after she died, the place was packed with friends. But strangely, I don't remember *who* exactly was there. Many of them didn't stay in my world for long after that. There were lots of cards and gifts. People sent these strange things to put out in my yard, ornaments to hang on the trees, little poems and angels and wind chimes. The wind chimes were the worst: every time I heard them chiming, I would think about Elizabeth and her being an angel out there. I don't know if other people find comfort in stuff like that, but I just found it creepy.

I smiled and thanked everyone who gave me those gifts, but I didn't want them. I put them all in a box, and they're still sitting in that box. I haven't opened it since, but maybe when I finish this book, it will be time for me to pull them out. Back then, I wasn't ready. I did what I had to do to put up a brave face and keep up with appearances. But it would still be many years until true healing came.

CHAPTER ELEVEN

Now

It wasn't until the spring of 2015, the second spring after Elizabeth passed, that I started to come alive again. What changed? The turning point was when I attended a grief group—put on by Children's Hospital and the Dana-Farber Cancer Institute—for parents who had lost their children through illness. The team at Children's had been trying to check in with me, calling and emailing, for a full year. But I just wasn't ready to talk or engage. I never answered, but to their credit, they kept trying. Then, one day, they sent me a note about the grief group.

Something about this invite struck a chord with me. I had almost tried something similar in the past, a group that the hospice had sent me to. But when I had gotten there, I couldn't do it. I had stopped and turned around—partly because I was terrified, but also because I realized I didn't want to hear about kids who had died from suicides and car accidents and the like. Those are terrible tragedies, of course, and I feel for the families, but I don't totally relate. They are a different kind of loss. It took me a while to figure this out: all loss is not the same.

Also, at that point, I was still just pissed off. Back then, the hospice group had given me a little pamphlet to read, and it was just crap. I wasn't in the right state of mind to hear that kind of stuff. And there was a certain value in my feeling pissed off. It made me happy in a way. It was a step in the right direction. At least when I was pissed off, I wasn't numb. But when the invitation to the new grief group arrived, it was the right circumstances and the right time. Don't get me wrong: I was still pissed, and I was definitely the angriest person in the group. I had the roughest edges. But the fact that the other parents had experienced the same kind of loss as me made a big difference. Those parents really touched me.

Not only that, but I got to reunite with some of the amazing hospital personnel who I had lost touch with: my social worker and my nurse practitioner. It felt good. Everyone else who had been part of my world—the network who used to help me take care of Elizabeth—was now gone, all the teachers, all the nurses. I had no more Perkins people, no more healthcare people. Everything was just over. Done. So to see the social worker and nurse practitioner felt like a glass of water in the desert. They were almost the only ones left who were still part of my connection with Elizabeth.

But of course, there was also Mark. He came with me to the grief group and was able to listen, but it was also the first time he was able to talk and be heard. Because he was the newcomer to our situation and the Best Supporting Actor, he never felt like he was able to claim the tragedy for himself. Finally, he was about to talk about it in that group, a full year and a half after Elizabeth died.

I never knew how he felt. Shame on me: I never asked him how he was doing. And even in that group, he talked maybe 20 percent of the time that I talked. But I got to have a little window into how he felt, particularly how hard it had been for him to see me so hurt and crushed by life. That group was so good for him; he got so much out of it. They were able to tell him things that I hadn't been able to say, like just what a wonderful person he was.

The grief group changed me, too. It was amazing in so many ways. We had different readings every week, and not all of them were slam-dunks, but they were always thought provoking. We also each got a little bottle and would add a new layer of colored sand each week, whatever color we chose. We did that for three months, and at the end, we all had these beautiful bottles: a collage of colorful sand in different layers and different colors.

The layers were not all the same depth, and they were a little intermingled. But the whole project connected with me, like I was developing my own new shoreline. As art, it was imperfect and always changing. Some weeks the sand would be black, some weeks pink or gray or brown or white. But I always felt like it represented what I was going through during this process of creating my new seascape.

It wasn't just about survival. It was a process of transformation. Through it all, I became something different and awesome. I still have the bottle to this day. It sits on top of my piano. Mark did one, too, and his sits next to mine.

It may have taken me a while to get in the groove of the grief group, but once I did, it was just what I needed, to let it all go and talk freely. It couldn't have happened earlier, until all the right pieces were in place. But now I had this group that I could really relate to, this tragic club of parents who had lost their children to disease. What an odd kind of community: it's a group you never expect to be a part of, and you certainly never want to join—but there it is. Thank God that they were there for me, that they understood and *wanted* to listen. I didn't have that anywhere else.

It marked the beginning of true healing for me. Finally, it was my time. I was ready for it, and I came out of the experience that spring with a renewed passion for my life.

Healing doesn't come in a linear fashion. Rather, it shows up in patches, like puffs of smoke. You catch a piece of it and start to feel whole again, but then it evaporates. There are starts and stops. But like the ocean, eventually the angry waves subside.

The next stage in my journey toward healing happened when my pastor invited us to Easter service that spring. I hadn't been going to church since Elizabeth had passed. I stopped going to mass. Part of it was I just couldn't bear being back in the same church where we had held the funeral. But the Easter service ended up helping me tremendously, and the reason for that is the pastor took the opportunity to talk to the congregation about Elizabeth. Our church is huge, and on Easter, it is *packed*. So this meant that hundreds of people got to hear about my daughter and her life story.

But it wasn't only Elizabeth's story that moved me that day. The pastor also told a tale that I'll never forget: about a boy who was sick and dying. I don't know exactly why, but the details of this story just hit me right in my emotional core. The boy's illness was causing him to lose his sight, and he kept asking his dad if it was morning yet. The sun hadn't arisen, but the boy didn't know that because he couldn't see. Eventually, he told his dad that he couldn't wait until he could greet the morning, and then he died.

In my Catholic tradition, we always talk about resurrection as being a new morning. In fact, I wrote that on Elizabeth's gravestone: that I can't wait until morning when I get to see her again.

I miss her so much. It's always there, the longing for the new morning that awaits me. It's like there's a hole in my body, a void that I carry around with me all the time.

Going to that Easter service brought me back to God. My season of healing was filling me with new energy, almost like a light switching on. It wasn't just the church service, or the grief group, it was everything. I was becoming ready to embrace life again. During this time, my mom also came back to live with us and help me with Caroline. I asked her to come back and help me, and she did. It was so good for us to be together as a family again. So nice for Caroline to have somebody else to lean on when I wasn't always able to be there for her. And for me, it was just very calming and peaceful to have my mom there. Sure, it's kind of weird when you're in your forties and you need your mommy. But it's pretty great when your mommy recognizes that and is there for you.

Then there was Mark, ever present, ever patient with me. He just waited for me to come back to life. He let me take as long as I needed. Earlier, when I had told him I wanted a divorce, he had just hugged me. He never left. It was like the conversation never happened. He continued to do laundry and take Caroline and do whatever needed to be done to make sure the family chugged along. He was rock steady. A miracle, really.

And what a contrast to Wayne, who was a disaster after Elizabeth died. There's no pleasant way to say this, but he was just *not* a help. He was the opposite. As I already mentioned, he almost didn't even come to see her before she died. Mark had to call, and we had to basically drag him up to Massachusetts.

Of course, it was sad and difficult for him as well. He's her father. He was in a lot of pain, too. But he didn't help make any decisions. Didn't participate. Didn't even do much to comfort Caroline. I think he was just shell-shocked.

Mark asked him to help pay for the funeral, but he said he didn't have any money to help. Eventually, his dad, Elizabeth's grandpa, sent us some money to help cover the funeral, which was very expensive, as funerals are. I had no idea of how pricey it would be, because I had never buried anyone. I don't remember the exact number, but I think the whole thing cost about $15,000. And that's not even including what we spent later on the gravestone, which was another few thousand dollars. Mark had to go into his savings to do it, because I was in bankruptcy at the time and broke.

A year and a half after Elizabeth died, Wayne started dragging up the past and grilling me about why I had stopped treating her, asking me for documentation and proof that it had been medically necessary. I could not believe what I was hearing from him. Why now? Why didn't he ask these questions *then*? He started calling all the doctors, the pediatrician, everyone at Children's Hospital. He reported to me that he'd been talking to his psychiatrist, and was on some kind of emotional journey, looking back through his past to uncover some truths. Or something.

Everyone at the hospital had the same response: they assured him that the whole clinical team had been in complete agreement about the decisions made when Elizabeth had passed. There was no question. Nothing for him to hang onto, if that's what he was looking for. You'd think he would have given up at that point, but no. He continued to press, and in such a thoughtless and accusatory way. I didn't get it at all. I mean, how was it helping? And why didn't he love me enough as the mother of his children to not put me through all that?

Eventually, I just told him: "Look, I'm not going to talk to you about this anymore. I'm not going to justify myself. I tried and tried to engage with you *when* she was dying. I called you during her hospital stays. You never came up when I asked you to come. You never wanted to know what was going on. I did the best I could. I'm done."

THE BEST I COULD

To this day, I still question all the things I've done. But I've gotten to a point where I can accept my humanity, flaws and all. I really am doing my best. I love my children. I love myself. I love my husband. I'm human and am going to continue to make mistakes. All I can do is ask for forgiveness from God, and the people around me, and just keep doing the best I can.

It took me a long time to get there. Man, did it take a long time. But if there's one thing that helped me get through, it's other moms and parents. Every step of the way, the breakthrough moments have been about those peer relationships, those connections with other people.

That, and prayer. It's not for everyone, but prayer has really helped me. I find myself calmed by it. I am so grateful that my pastor invited us to that Easter service after Elizabeth passed, because it got me back into church. After that, I kept going back. I would go to mass, and the rituals of that ceremony were just so calming and peaceful for me. I would cry every time, but it was good. A good cry. Cathartic. If felt good to give it all up to God.

Nowadays, I feel like I'm finally back out there. The practice has exploded over the last three years; we've tripled our business. Best of all, the work genuinely fulfills me. I love going to my office every day. What a contrast to those first few weeks after Elizabeth died, when I would spend hours crying on my desk. I think about that dark time, and it just makes me appreciate more how much I enjoy my job now. I literally can't wait to get to work. I'm so happy there, even when it's challenging. I also do tons of speaking these days at parent groups and other special needs-related venues. But it didn't just happen; I deliberately pushed myself back out there, onto those stages.

After Elizabeth died, no one called me with those kinds of invitations anymore. They were afraid to ask because of everything I'd been through. So when I was ready, I had to be proactive and make those calls and emails. I would reach out and say: "Hey, I'm back. Let's get together." It had the effect of letting everyone know that I was okay, and that it was fine to call me.

Hey, I could've chosen to be angry again, angry that I had to be the one to make the first move and reconnect with people. But I just wasn't. My anger was gone. I was just happy to be back. The old Annie would have thought of it as a burden: *why should I have to go through this and reach out to people?* I would have been pissed off that people weren't doing what I expected them to do. But it wasn't like that anymore.

Now, every time I do a talk, I talk about Elizabeth. At first, it was too difficult to discuss. But I actually love talking about her, and how she shaped my life, and made me such a good mom—and such a good advocate for others. I can't really explain what changed; all I can say is that there's no longer this huge bubble of pain that wells up. People also respond differently to me now. They have a different reaction than they used to, because I'm talking about the experience in a loving way, not from a place of anger. They can tell that things have changed for me, so they don't feel uncomfortable anymore.

It's still pretty rare that people will ask me, unsolicited, about Elizabeth, or about how I'm doing as a parent who's lost their child. I've learned that it's a very small, select group of people who can talk honestly about child-loss, who I can share with and say, for example: "Ugh, today is not a good day, I had a terrible dream," or "It's her birthday," or whatever it may be. I know where I can get that kind of support from, and I know where I can't. And that's fine. I know myself better than ever. I still grieve. I still have my bad days.

The pain never fully goes away, whether it's the pain of losing a child or just the pain that goes along with raising a child who has disabilities. All I can say is that for me, and for many people I've met on my journey, it does get better.

Epilogue

SEEING BUTTERFLIES

In 2018, I began writing this book. It felt so right, and I was so happy to be doing it. I was finally ready to tell Elizabeth's story. It felt like a continuation, an extension, of what I had been doing at my talks to groups—speaking about Elizabeth and telling her story from this new place of deep love and acceptance.

In summer of 2018, I met my editor at Prospect Park in Brooklyn, New York, where he lives. It was our first time meeting in person. He brought along his own seven-year-old son, who is on the autism spectrum and has a seizure disorder. It was a beautiful day, sunny and warm but not humid, and we met in the big playground behind the concert bandshell. Kids of all ages and backgrounds were running, climbing, swinging, playing in the sprinklers.

My editor's son was a delight: he didn't have many words—he is severely speech-delayed—but he gave me a sweet smile and a high-five. And what I remember most about that day was what happened after we said our goodbyes. My husband, Mark, and I were walking through the park when we saw a yellow butterfly. I commented on it, about how fitting it was to see the beautiful creature at that exact moment, given Elizabeth's own love of butterflies. But then what happened was truly amazing: it was as if this butterfly *knew*. It stayed with us, landing sweetly on my arm, and then flitting all around us for the next ten minutes.

What's really remarkable is that ever since that day, I've seen yellow butterflies *everywhere*. It's like I tapped into something, and now the yellow butterfly population of the world is drawn to me. Caroline keeps noticing it, too. We had one get into the house a couple of weeks ago. Caroline took a picture of it and texted it to me.

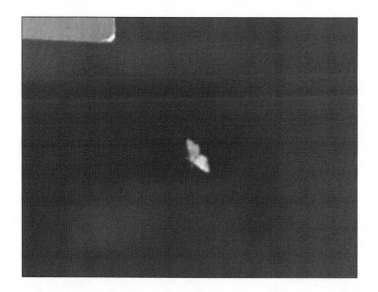

As for Caroline, she graduated from high school, and her last two years of school she really got focused and did exceptionally well in her classes. She became interested in pursuing science and medicine. It's a fact that a disproportionate number of siblings go into the "helping" professions, such as medicine, science, social work. This year, my heart burst with pride as I dropped her off at college to study biochemistry. I know she still struggles with all that has happened to her in her life. But at least now we are both far enough in our healing journey that we can talk to each other about us and about Elizabeth.

We had a party for Caroline's graduation from high school, and a little yellow butterfly made an appearance there, too—floating around all over the place. I went over to it and said, "Hi, Elizabeth. I'm so glad you could come." Far-fetched? Maybe. But I just feel like Elizabeth wants me to know that she's still with me, and also that I'm doing a good job. Like, "Way to go, mom."

That's what I felt when we were walking back through the park in Brooklyn. As the butterfly danced around me, I took it as a sign. She was telling me that I'm doing good, that the book is a good idea—and that she's happy. I looked at the butterfly and thought to myself, *Hi, Elizabeth.*

About the Author

ANNETTE HINES is a founding partner of the Special Needs Law Group of Massachusetts. She brings personal experience to her practice as the mother of two daughters, one of whom passed away from mitochondrial disease in 2013. This deep personal understanding of special needs fuels her passion for quality special needs planning and drives her dedication to the practice. Recognized as a Distinguished Citizen by ARC Massachusetts and cited for public service by both the Massachusetts State Senate and House of Representatives, Ms. Hines works tirelessly on behalf of people with disabilities.

Made in the USA
Middletown, DE
08 July 2022

68806401R00125